EMILY POST'S
ADVICE FOR EVERY
DINING OCCASION

EMILY POST'S
ADVICE FOR EVERY DINING OCCASION

ELIZABETH L. POST

HarperCollinsPublishers

HarperCollins books may be purchased for educational, business, or sales promotional use. For information, please write to Special Markets Department, HarperCollins Publishers, Inc., 10 East 53rd Street, New York, New York 10022.

FIRST EDITION

Designed by C. Linda Dingler
Illustrations by Jim Cozza

Library of Congress Cataloging-in-Publication Data
Post, Elizabeth L.
    Emily Post's advice for every dining occasion / Elizabeth L. Post.
    p. cm.
    ISBN 0-06-270099-5
    1. Table etiquette. I. Title. II. Title: Table manners for today.
    BJ2041.P67 1994
    395'.54—dc20   93-32393

97 98 ❖/RRD 10 9 8 7 6 5 4 3

CONTENTS

INTRODUCTION

Today there are few moments other than mealtime when families are able to spend time together recounting the day's activities. How sad. Yet it would be sadder still to lose this last vestige of family time only to share meals served on snack trays around the television set, eat meals on the run or have dinners where family members wolf down their food and leap up to engage in other activities.

If your dinner table has become a typically frenzied place, underpopulated and where eating is overly hurried, read on. It is never too late to start a new tradition, or revive a dormant one to make mealtimes warm, well-mannered, happy times to gather. While there is nothing wrong with an occasional Chinese take-out dinner with white cartons right on the table in front of the television, there is a lot wrong with children growing up thinking that this is all there is to eating. When children are taught correct table manners from a very young age they grow up being more comfortable in any dining situation than do their peers who lack these same skills.

Whether your family consists of two people or a houseful, try to make at least one meal a week an oasis for the family, a relaxing and gracious time where focusing on one another is the priority. Making it a feast for the eye as well as for the palate helps, as does a shared appreciation for mealtime manners. Practiced diligently at home, courtesy and manners quickly become a habit. When elbows aren't allowed on the table at your home, they won't be placed there in someone else's. When food is always chewed with the mouth closed at home, it is never on view in public. When family members pause to swallow a mouthful of food before conversation continues at your dinner table, they'll naturally do the same at a restaurant.

Think about an annoying habit someone you know has. Most likely it is unconscious.

A friend is astonished to find out that he jiggles his leg up and down every time he sits down.

Your daughter denies vehemently saying "Ya know" seven times in every sentence; but you know because it is so distracting that you count when she talks instead of trying to listen to what she says.

Your son ends every sentence with a question mark, even when what he is saying is not a question. "We went to the video store? And there was this really gross looking guy? And he looked like he hadn't had a bath for a week?" This makes you wild because it forces you to respond "uh-huh, yes, uh-huh" to every single sentence he utters, until you stop listening to him, too.

And you have no idea that you twist your hair around your finger when you are nervous.

In the same way, people wave their forks in the air as they talk, talk with food in their mouths and tap their spoons on the table without even knowing they are doing it. These things are done without thought because they have become habits. Bad habits. Once learned, they are hard to unlearn. While they may be overlooked in private, these bad habits can be annoying, embarrassing or even rude in public.

To make sure that you and your family have good manners in public you must practice good manners at home. This includes *consideration for others* (no rude remarks, learning to be a good listener), *thoughtfulness* (not leaving used tissues on the bathroom vanity); holding a chair for Mom when she is being seated at the table); and *kindness* (volunteering to set the table; asking someone else about his or her day). Throughout this book you'll find the essentials of table manners and mealtime etiquette for every dining occasion. Here are the guidelines for everything from dining at home to eating out, from being served at a formal dinner to helping yourself at a buffet restaurant, from the proper way to set the table for a picnic to the number of knives in a formal place setting, from learning how to eat tacos and tortillas to using snail tongs, from dealing with the maitre d's to accepting an invitation to dinner. In short, you'll find everything that helps you be comfortable and unselfconscious in all situations.

Elizabeth L. Post
1994

1

At Home:

Making Mealtime Memorable

We shouldn't save our best manners for the outside world—
surely the people with whom we live deserve our best efforts.

SETTING YOUR STANDARDS

Whether you or your family's at-home table manners need a
small tune-up or a major overhaul, the process need not be
unpleasant. Many adults today tell of childhood memories of
being poked in the arm with a fork when their elbows were on
the table and being knuckled in the back when they were
slouching; of being forced to sit at the table by the hour until
every single Brussels sprout was eaten; or of being sent to their
rooms for directing rude splatting noises at their brother in the
middle of dinner. While their lessons were learned, they can be
learned just as easily with gentle reminders and with simple
communication. More often than not, there are very good reasons for rules of behavior, which, once understood, make sense
and are not hard to remember.

When your concern is teaching table manners, keep in mind
that standards should be age-appropriate. A young child, the
moment he begins chewing, can understand that this should be
done with the mouth closed. He has difficulty keeping his

elbows at his side when he is cutting his food, however, because small motor skills take a while to develop. When you remember to make allowances for skill development and understanding, it is not difficult to make good table manners lifelong habits. It is easier when the environment is attractive, when the menu is pleasing, and when the company is congenial—the same ingredients for any dinner party you would have for guests.

The Environment

Make your own standard one that is dedicated to setting a pretty table. It doesn't take that much more time to use place mats, to fold napkins, and to set attractive places for family meals.

If children are assigned the chore of setting the table, you can even encourage them to think of centerpieces, choose background music, and find a long-forgotten dish for the pickles.

Make an extra effort for holidays, whether they be Christmas or Passover feasts or those you make special just for fun, like a celebration of Groundhog Day or Peter Rabbit's birthday. Again, involve children in thinking of ways to make the table especially festive. If a twelve-year-old has finished her homework and is restlessly awaiting dinner, have her cut and fold paper to make place cards. Even if everyone always sits in the same chair for dinner, it is fun to have this addition to the table once in a while and it introduces the concept, opening you to talk about places you have been where place cards were used and how they were used.

A big part of the environment is the room you eat in. If you have a dining room, use it once in a while; don't always eat in the kitchen. If the kitchen is your primary dining spot, then be sure counters aren't heaped with pots and pans and dirty dishes. Make the space around the table inviting, too.

Equally as important, the environment should allow you to

focus on one another. Only once in a great while should the television be on. Only when something is terribly urgent should protracted telephone calls be allowed.

One young family I know uses dinner time to introduce a variety of classical music as a background to conversation. Practically by osmosis, the children learn to identify major themes and composers, and often the music itself presents a conversational topic. Involving children in choosing music is another way to lead them to a full participation in the dinner hour. If your music collection is wide, help them choose something fitting: the *Hungarian Rhapsodies* when you are having Hungarian stew; Italian mountain songs when you are serving lasagna; a romantic medley on Valentine's Day.

The Menu

A dinner menu will seldom please all of the people all of the time. With children it's a topic that lends itself to a great deal of "hate" venting, as in, "I *hate* peas!" and "I *hate* meat!" If you are the only one thinking up menu ideas night after night, these comments are as frustrating as they are rude. It is tiring to work hard to feed your family creatively and well only to have one family member or another sound off every night.

An end run around this problem is to assign menu planning to others every now and then. Periodically ask your spouse and your children or the primary complainer to come up with a week's worth of dinner menus. With the children, review the menus for balance and nutrition. Explain why mashed potatoes and spaghetti at one dinner doesn't work. When youngsters learn it is not easy to plan a satisfactory menu they will develop an appreciation of your efforts, and will be less critical. When dinner is just something that appears on the table, very little thought is given to how it got there and why. Giving in to their special requests occasionally also makes them feel more involved in the process and gives them a greater interest in the meals. When one has actually worked to plan what that dinner is, a new appreciation dawns.

Congenial Company

Creating a warm and inviting environment for family mealtime helps ensure that you have at least one time and place a day to focus on one another, to share feelings, ideas and thoughts and to do something as a unit. Sharing a meal is just the beginning. The rest of it is helping everyone at the table to remember the manners of consideration. The dinner table is often the place where children learn about taking turns to talk and where, with everyone gathered, they can share their greatest triumphs of the day, as well as their anxieties and problems. It should be a place of praise, laughter and happiness. It should never be a place of tension and anger.

My rule has always been that fights, grudges, disagreements and anger do not sit at my table. It is literally unhealthy; chronic stomach problems are often traced to the dinner table. When tension reigns, digestion suffers. More than that, it is unfair to the cook, unkind to others, basically selfish and certainly unpleasant.

Even if dinner has to be delayed a half-hour to resolve conflict so that it doesn't come to the table, it is worth it. Using dinner time to be unpleasant can become a habit just as quickly as talking with a full mouth.

If dinner table conversation is nonexistent or mumbled between mouthfuls, it is time to change your family's ways. Begin by asking questions that cannot be answered "fine," "yes" or "no." Don't ask, "Did you have a good day in school?" Ask instead, "What are you studying in science right now?" Then ask a few questions about that topic. Ask, "What was the best thing that happened to you today?" and then ask why. Don't ask, "How was lunch today with Larry?" Say instead, "What is the Black Bass Grill like?" or "What did you like best about the restaurant?" This is not to assume that your only role is to quiz the family. You should be prepared to share a story as well, preferably one of interest to most of the people at the table.

Try to encourage a discussion of something that is happening in the world; talk about an editorial in the newspaper and ask everyone else what his or her opinion is. Create a "word of the week" game and assign each person the responsibility for finding a word, looking it up and teaching it to everyone else. Then have each person use the word in a sentence during dinner throughout the week.

Buy a book on the derivation of phrases or sayings and every so often ask someone to find a really interesting one and teach the others all about it. For example, in keeping with the dinner-table theme, you could describe why we drink a "toast" to someone. And so you can try this out tonight, here's why.

The custom of drinking a toast to the good health of another began in ancient times. In the days of Shakespeare, a piece of toasted bread was put in the tankard before wine or ale was poured into it. This toast allegedly improved the taste; it also collected any sediment and impurities at the bottom of the tankard. The drink, therefore, became a toast. The health part comes next. A little of the wine or ale was poured into the host's glass and then into the guest's glass from the same pitcher before anyone drank, just in case one or the other had poison on the mind. Since both would drink from the same source, it was a pretty sure bet that there was no poison—after all, who would look to poison himself! Before drinking, the two, or the group, would clink tankards and say, "To your good health," which they could say with some certainty, having passed the poison test.

BASIC GUIDELINES

The truth is that most children *want* to know how to do things properly. They dread embarrassment, wither at the thought of seeming foolish or ignorant and feel very good about themselves, indeed, when they know how to do something the right way. As long as you don't make the teaching of basic dining guidelines rigid and grim, the entire process can be fun for everyone. And don't forget to explain *why* things are done certain ways. Knowing why makes remembering easier, and children are literal and logical so if something makes sense they'll make it their own.

Please do keep age and ability in mind as you teach. Little children don't know how not to burp loudly and actually find the sound hilarious. Glowers and admonishments from you are inappropriate; explaining that they must excuse themselves if they do burp is appropriate. Small ones need bibs, because getting food from dish to mouth is a very hard thing to do. Scolding for drips and spills is inappropriate at this point. Older children, who are rushing, gobbling or not paying attention don't need bibs, (and should not have napkins tucked into their shirts); they do need to be helped to slow down and learn how much a fork or spoon can logically hold.

Posture

Remember that when your feet do not touch the floor it is hard to hold yourself in a comfortably upright position. As much as is possible, however, children should learn to sit straight at the table. Older children and teens should be reminded to keep their backs against the back of the chair. If they persist in slouching, demonstrate the difference yourself by hunching over your plate and sitting straight. Tell them how much more attractive they look sitting up straight.

Elbows, Hands and Arms

Many years ago there was a rhyme for children about elbows: "Mabel, Mabel, brave and able, keep your elbows off the table." As silly as this sounds, it teaches in a light way. Teens, particularly, will lean forward with their entire arms around their dinner plate. Why is this wrong? It causes slouching. It takes up table space. It gets in the way of table service at a formal party or restaurant. It is impolite.

Elbows also must not energetically pump as food is cut. As soon as a child has mastered the skill of fork, knife and cutting her own food, you should help her learn to do so with her elbows as close to her sides as possible. Why? Because, although your table may have three feet between diners, most dining occasions see people sitting only a foot and one half apart, and flying elbows bump neighbors. Why should she care when there is plenty of room at home? Because if she learns to cut this way, and also to eat this way (elbows should not be sticking out, parallel to the floor as spoon or fork travel from plate to mouth), she will cut and eat this way all the time and appear boorish and ill-mannered. It becomes a habit.

It is permissable before the meal starts or between courses to put your elbows on the table so that you can lean forward to speak to the people across the table.

Hands should lie loosely in the lap when they are not being used or rest on the table at the wrist only. If a child learns to cut and eat American-style, where the knife is put down and the fork is transferred to the right hand, the left hand should be on the lap after the transfer, not on the table. Hands should also be on the lap anytime eating is not taking place, never on the table, never in the air, never thumping and tapping or twirling forks in the air. In fact, if they are in the lap, none of these annoying little things can take place.

Cutting Food

At first telling, it seems illogical to teach a child that after years of having all his food cut up at once so he could eat it, he now must only cut one or two bites at a time. The reason: It looks very messy to have a plateful of cut-up food, it simply is impolite to do it all at once and it also speeds the cooling of hot foods. Why is it all right for a two-year old? Because she can't cut her own food and is learning to manage eating and gain independence before she can care about manners. And because cutting one piece at a time would mean the designated cutter would have to stand through the meal waiting for the child to finish each bite.

How Much Is Enough?

When serving dishes are passed, children can be uncertain as to how much of any food they should take. Shy children may take only two French fries, thinking it would seem greedy to take more; more confident children may scoop half the contents of the bowl onto their plates just because they love them. It is easier to demonstrate what a *normal* or *modest* helping is than to describe it, and to point out the logic of being able to look at a platter of lamb chops and gauge that two per person have been prepared so that one does not help oneself to three at first pass.

Take Human Bites!

Children need help understanding how much is enough when it comes to a forkful or a spoonful of food. Enough is an amount that fits within the bowl of the spoon; that rests without precarious balancing on the tines of the fork; and that fits into a partially opened mouth. Too much hangs over the sides of utensils and fills the mouth completely. Too much is dangerous—it can cause choking and prohibits adequate chewing. It is unsightly—it makes the cheeks bulge and prevents the mouth from closing. And it is unnecessary—gulping and gobbling are neither attractive nor polite.

Chewing

Food must be chewed thoroughly before it is swallowed. If it isn't, damage can be done to the digestive system. The manners part? It is done with the mouth closed. Why? Because it is disgusting to see someone's partially chewed food. It is not a pleasant sight. In the same vein, food must be swallowed before the mouth is opened to talk.

A mouthful should be swallowed before a beverage is brought to the lips, unless the mouthful is so astonishingly hot that immediate relief from cold milk or water is necessary to prevent a burn. The reason for the swallow-before-drinking rule is that one could choke on unchewed food washed down the throat. The other reason is that if some of the food in the mouth floats into the glass it looks extremely unappetizing.

Something Yucky

When a child puts something in his mouth that he finds terribly unpleasant, he must be taught how to remove it. Little children tend to spit things out. This ceases to be cute after the age of three. Older children should practice removing unwanted food by pushing it onto a spoon or fork or into their cupped fingers and lowering it to their plate. Although it seems neater to simply push it from the mouth into a napkin, which is marginally all right when the napkin is paper and can be thrown right out, knowing how to transfer from mouth to fork or spoon will come in handy when they are in a situation where cloth napkins are used. And one does not spit food into a cloth napkin.

Which Fork?

According to my mail, one of the greatest anxieties suffered by young and old alike occurs when they are faced, for the first time, with an array of flatware and haven't a clue which fork or knife or spoon to use. This is not a scary thing. Assuming that the table is set correctly, the utensils at the outside, farthest away from the plate, are the ones that are used first. The rule on how to begin is "from the outside in" and it is based on logic: the outside utensils are the easiest to pick up first. If we had to pull from the inside or the middle, we might knock all the other utensils awry and leave an odd space near the plate. *(Please see page 78 for a diagram of how many utensils might be presented at one time and how they are arranged.)*

Excuse Me

Hiccups, burps and other strange noises sometimes happen. It would be a rare individual who never emitted any of these sounds. People are understanding as long as the offender immediately excuses himself. Children should learn, as early as they understand and speak in sentences, to say "Excuse me," when the strange noise is coming from them. And not to howl with laughter when it is coming from someone else.

Spoon Noises

As delicious as the last possible taste of ice cream in the bottom of the bowl might be, it is impolite to scrape loudly with the spoon to try to get it all. Why? It is an unpleasant sound and usually requires that people raise their voices to talk above it.

Eating Noises

Eating should not be a noisy undertaking. Slurping, crunching and lip smacking are not considered polite. Often a young person has to be taught how to take just enough soup on the spoon, how to test it to be sure it isn't too hot, and then how to tip the spoon into the mouth so it is poured, not sucked or slurped. As with many of the topics here, food noises can actually become habits if no one points out to the oblivious offender that he is making them.

Humming and Singing

One neither hums nor sings at the dinner table, no matter how tunefully one may be able to do either. It is irritating, and it interferes with conversation. Children who hum may not be aware that they are doing it. Gently ask them to stop then attempt to engage them in the general conversation—the humming is a clear sign that they are *not* paying attention!

Hats and Shirts

Hats are not worn indoors at the table. Even though it may seem as though it is a permanent part of your son's head, his carefully molded baseball cap must come off when he sits down. With the exception of small boys in fast-food restaurants who may keep their baseball caps on, hats are not indoor wear, and they are not table wear.

Shirts, on the other hand, are always worn at the table. A bare torso is not acceptable, and neither is a bare chest that can be seen through an unbuttoned shirt. The day may be hot and your son may have spent it shirtless, but when he comes inside to dinner he must cover up. This particular guideline has to do with sanitation and overall attractiveness.

Interrupting

As during any other time, no one should interrupt another at the dinner table unless it is to say that the stove is on fire or to report another emergency. The table is often the one place where children learn the art and skill of conversational exchange, and they should learn to wait their turn to speak, to say "Excuse me, Mom," if they have something they absolutely must say, and to apologize if they inadvertently interrupt or begin speaking at the same time as someone else does.

Please Pass. . .

One of the most basic rules of mealtime is not to reach for something clearly out of reach. Children need to learn that if the desired item is not directly in front of them, they must ask for it.

Not as in, "Gimme the butter," but as in "Jerry, would you please pass the butter?"

When others seem to be engaged in a conversation that is endless and your mashed potatoes are growing cold and you want to add butter in time for it to melt, it is all right to ask the person who is nearest the butter to pass it.

Condiments

Children may be used to adding pools of ketchup to their plates at a fast-food restaurant or at home when burgers and fries are the menu, but they should be taught that this cannot be done in someone else's home. Why? Because it indicates that the food needs to be smothered in additives to be palatable. When condiments are on the table, it is acceptable to take a small amount, spooning or pouring them on the side or rim of the plate. It is not acceptable to bury food in sauces.

Napkins

Napkins belong in the lap when not in use. When in use, they should be used to pat, not rub, the mouth, and to clean the hands. Most families use paper napkins, which is convenient. They should not be thrown onto the dinner plate when dinner is over, but smoothed slightly and placed on the table. When cloth napkins are used and each child has his or her own napkin ring, the napkin is folded lightly and replaced in the ring if it is to be used again.

Chairs

It is frequently necessary to remind taller, older children, whose feet reach the floor, that they should immediately cease and desist tipping their chairs back. In addition to the general irritation it causes to have someone rocking back and forth at the table, chairs are not made to be tipped onto two legs and will eventually break.

Fingers or Forks?

There are a few foods that are eaten with the hands at home, but must be tackled with a knife and fork in the greater world. If fried chicken, for example, is eaten with the fingers at your house (which is perfectly correct), you should once or twice have everyone try eating it with a fork and knife, just so they know how to do so. The same is true of entire chops—if your family picks up the whole chop at home, have everyone cut some of the meat off the chop with a knife and fork, just for the practice. And while on the subject of practicing, neatly eating spaghetti and other long pasta should be practiced at home, too. Slurping strands from plate to mouth is not acceptable. *(Please see Chapter Four for tips on tricky foods and how to eat them.)*

Fun Food

Food is not something to play with, although most people make airplane noises to get babies to open their mouths for that first shocking taste of beets or pulverized chicken, and continue to play food "games" to get children to try new foods.

As long as this practice eventually stops, it seems to set no lifelong patterns, but it must stay at home. A child over the age of five should know that he cannot make a tower of his carrot cubes when dining out, or arrange his peas around the edge of his plate, even though he is making a fence to keep the potatoes in.

Spills

If spills didn't happen, carpet manufacturers would not constantly be seeking new, spill-resistant fibers. Unless a child deliberately throws something on the floor, an action requiring a serious response, no parent should become apoplectic over an accidental spill. Stop and think—if it were a guest who spilled something would you have a fit and castigate him for his clumsiness? I would hope not. Family members are people, too, and deserve the same understanding reaction that you would offer to your guests.

Anyone who does spill, however, should take quick action to clean up. Help children know how to help. Whether the cleaning agent is soap and water or club soda and whether the action required is blotting with a towel or scrubbing with a brush, the spiller should help clean up the mess. And then hypothetical situations should be discussed so everyone knows what to do when a dreaded spill occurs in someone else's house or in a restaurant.

In another's home, the person who spills should immediately apologize and ask where to find towels or a sponge. The hostess may prefer to take care of it herself, but the offer should be made.

In a restaurant, the waiter or waitress should be called and he or she will take care of the problem, either by covering a spill on the table with another cloth, or by sweeping, mopping or picking up the accident.

If possible, share one of your own spill stories; relate how embarrassed you were, and what you did. This reassures children that their world will not end when it happens to them. Older children and teens should be taught to offer to repair or replace anything spilled on or broken—not in the middle of a dinner party, but during a quiet moment with the hostess. And they should be sure to apologize once again. The kind parent, as would the kind host, will surely say, "It doesn't matter at all—I don't want you to give it another thought."

Seconds

When at home, it is fine to ask for a second helping. If none is left, no one is embarrassed, and the cook makes a mental note to prepare a little more next time. When out, however, one may not ask. If there is more, it will be offered and etiquette says that one must wait until it is. If there is no more, the hostess may be embarrassed.

May I Please Be Excused?

Everyone, from the very young to the very old, must ask to be excused. The question is asked of the hostess (Mom), if she is at the table, and is asked of the hostess (whomever) when out, not of Mom.

Ideally, if permission is granted, this query is followed by thanks. And a compliment to the meal is always welcome. When children are invited to have dinner at a friend's house, it is important to remind them of this: "Thank you, Mrs. Capasso, that was a delicious dinner," or words to that effect. And how nice if that is said at home once in a while, too, as in, "Thank you, Mom, that was a great dinner!" If no one has thought to say that to Mom lately, it should be practiced. It is a guideline that adds a social grace and poise to a child, or an adult, who has enjoyed a meal at someone else's table.

PLEASE AND THANK YOU

Please and *Thank you* are still the "magic" words, and you will be doing your child a favor if you insist that she use them until they become a habit. The dinner table is the perfect place to practice. Everyone likes to be appreciated, and "thank you" is the accepted way of showing appreciation. When someone passes the butter, the automatic response should be "thank you."

"Please" turns a demand into a request and indicates an option—it turns an unpopular request into a more palatable one. "Would you please clear the table?" elicits a friendlier response than does "Clear the table now."

The essential requirement in teaching your child to use the "magic" words is—use them yourself. Too many parents say, "Get the mayonnaise from the refrigerator," "Hand me that bowl," or "Don't tip your chair," without even a "Would you" or a "Please." They then consistently respond to their youngsters' demands by saying, "What do you say?" or "If you say *please.*" You must do this constantly with both *please* and *thank you* when children are small, as a reminder, but they will get the point much faster if you practice what you preach and this courtesy is commonplace in your house and at your table.

SAYING GRACE

Another "thank you" at the table is that given through prayer. In many homes, grace is said before the meal begins. Some people remain standing until grace is said; others are seated. Many families hold hands around the table; others fold their hands in their laps or on the edge of the table. Often families say a prayer together. Sometimes one person says the grace.

Even if your family does not say grace, your children should know what it means and what to do when at another's table where it is said. They needn't feel forced to participate, but they should know to sit quietly and respect the beliefs of others.

If your family does say grace, you might occasionally ask your children if they would like to lead the family in grace, or help them to learn a different prayer every now and then.

When a visitor is with you, he or she should not be put on the spot and asked to lead the grace unless he or she is a rabbi or a minister.

LIKES AND DISLIKES

Did you really like mushrooms when you were seven? Or broccoli, or turnips? Probably not. It is also probable that even when forced to gag them down before being allowed to leave the table, you didn't like them any better.

Children today have the same aversions, which may include things that surprise you, like hot dogs and hamburgers or strawberry ice cream. How you deal with these dislikes at home is your choice. My feeling is that asking, not forcing, a child to take a minute taste of something that is served, every time it is served, at least expands his horizons for the future. Some parents cook entirely separate meals for children who express displeasure with the meatloaf and baked potato dinner that is being served that night. This is spoiling the child and should not be done. Far better to insist that what is served is what is to be eaten, or even to permit children to eat only what they like from the dinner, providing no alternatives. It is prudent to check with your pediatrician as to nutrient needs for your child if you have a truly picky eater, using whatever he or she says as your personal guideline for dealing with dietary questions.

What we are discussing here, however, are the manners related to refusing a food. Whining about food and stubbornly refusing to eat something just because one doesn't particularly like it is not to be condoned, either at home or elsewhere. There are some things, however, that a child simply cannot eat or genuinely does not care for and he or she has a real problem, away from home particularly, when that is what is offered. You must distinguish the difference with your children, explaining that usually they are expected to eat what is put in front of them away from home, no matter what your rules are at home.

It is important to give a child of any age the skills needed to decline and accept politely, whether having Sunday dinner at your mother's or an after-school snack at a friend's house, and to make a decision when offered a choice. Knowing these skills also prepares him or her to be a thoughtful future host or hostess.

Very young children must learn that they cannot make rude noises or grimacing faces when presented with something they truly do not like. The first response is, "No, thank you"; the second, if pushed by a well-meaning adult, is, "I'm sorry, but I can't eat octopus." If the adult cannot leave well enough alone and persists or asks why or tries to cajole, the third response is, "Because it makes my stomach upset," or, "Because the taste bothers me," or, "Because I haven't learned to like the way it tastes, yet."

Older children and teens should be able to say, "No, thank you, very much," without having to give further explanations.

When a child of any age has a health-related problem, he shouldn't feel forced to explain it. A child with diabetes who cannot have food with sugar should be taught to say, "Thank you, but I can't eat sugar." If the offerer is rude enough to ask why, and your child feels the reason is none of her business, he may merely say, "Because my doctor said I can't." That should be unarguable. Naturally the parent of a small child should be specific with an adult caretaker, whether babysitter or mother of the child's friend, when health risks are related to eating.

A child who is sticking to a strict diet, a difficult thing for a child to do at all, should understand the limits of the diet and communicate them to a host or hostess. Only an obtuse adult would say, "Oh, just one little piece of cake won't hurt you!"

The truly awkward position of being at a friend's for dinner and disliking or being unable to eat anything on the table is a tough one for a young person to deal with. It is never too early to learn to take little portions of everything and hopefully find one thing, whether a piece of bread or the salad, to eat, slowly, so as not to outpace the others at the table. Eating *all* the bread, however, is not polite, even if it is the only thing on the table she likes.

If a thoughtful hostess notices that a youngster is not eating, she may, without making a major production out of it, quietly say, "I guess these aren't your favorite things—how about a peanut butter sandwich, instead?" And the child is free to say, "thanks, that would be great." Having a guest go hungry at the table does not make the hostess any happier than it does the child. Let your children know that if offered a preferable alternative, it is all right to accept it. If no alternative is offered but a hostess comments that a child "hasn't touched his liver and onions!" it is better for him to say, "I'm just not hungry, I guess," than to say "I *hate* liver." The truth is, unless the hostess is prepared to offer an alternative, she shouldn't turn the spotlight on the child who is not eating.

TRY IT, YOU'LL LIKE IT!

Helping a child learn to refuse something politely should not take the place of helping him expand his taste horizons. When a child is permitted to eat nothing but grilled cheese sandwiches and drink nothing but apple juice for fourteen years, (the case with one child I know), it is likely that he will never become an experimental eater, will never know how interesting different taste experiences can be and will always be limited to just a few main staples in his diet.

Every time you try something new, make sure your children try it, too. Just a little taste. When asked what the food is, don't respond "Just try it." Give the name of the food, anything you might know about it and if possible relate it to a food they already know. "It's arugula, a salad green common in the Mediterranean. It gives the salad an interesting mustard flavor." Finding out that something is actually very good gives them the courage to try the next new food experience you provide, and then the next. Finding out that they don't like something right now does not mean, you should explain, that they won't like it in the future. Your positive encouragement is all that is needed.

My one caution is that you should refrain from making a major issue out of food. As with anger and tension at the table, a total focus on food can have a damaging impact. I do not believe food should be offered as treats, either. Think about what you are implying when you say, "If you finish your spinach, you can have ice cream. If you don't, you can't." You are implying that spinach is bad and ice cream is good.

Offering food to console is another action to reconsider. Research shows that children who were comforted with food—"I'm sorry you are sad about losing that game...I'll bet a little chocolate cake would cheer you up!"—will turn to food, more likely than not, when they are depressed as adults, too. The more depressed they are, the more they eat, the heavier they get, the more depressed they get, and so on. It is far better, in my opinion, to console with a hug, a kiss and an activity.

Food, after all, is just the fuel for our systems, not the fulcrum of our lives. Rather than making it an obsessive fixation, we simply hope it is always delicious, always nutritious and presented and eaten with lovely manners which make it all the more enjoyable.

WHAT WOULD YOU LIKE?

Another obstacle for children and teens to overcome is that of dealing with choices. They need to practice responding to the question, "Do you want cola or orange soda?" with an answer other than, "I don't care...what are you having?" If they do have a preference, you need to let them know that it is all right, not rude, to express it. If they don't, they should make their own choice anyway.

They also need to know that, because they are uncomfortable, they shouldn't just say "No, thank you," or "Nothing for me, thanks," when they really are thirsty. Most people are more comfortable when others *accept* their hospitality, even when they don't exactly know how to offer it. An enthusiastic, "Yes, please! That would be great!!" or "Yes, please! I would love a soda," is most satisfactory and makes the host feel that he or she is doing a good job.

I will never forget the story of a friend in New York City, many years ago, who was instructed by his parents to always refuse any offer the first time it was made, because it was the "polite" thing to do. People would always offer a second time, or say, "Are you sure?" or, "Oh, try just a little," after which it was all right to accept, they told him. Traveling for two hours by subway and ferry to visit in Staten Island, and feeling very hungry, he was offered refreshment upon arrival. "No, thank you," he politely answered. And that was it. After a two-hour visit and another two hours traveling back home, he was famished and furious. And he learned an important lesson. The polite host and hostess do *not* insist or force food on anyone, respecting their refusal the first time. Your children need to know this and learn to be comfortable accepting hospitality when it is offered.

Most people are stymied by the question, "What would you like?" if they don't know what the choices are. Since the question is inadequate, children should know that it is perfectly all right to respond, "What are you offering?"

When the question is, "Can I get you something to drink," it is equally all right to say, "Yes, thank you, that would be nice," and wait for a list of what is available. If no list is forthcoming and the question becomes, "What would you like?" the answer again may be, "What are you offering?"

Both of these awkward situations are wonderful lessons to children for when it is their turn to be a host or hostess. Properly asked, the question is, "We have orange juice, cola, lemonade and water. . . which may I get for you?"

SETTING LIMITS

Conversation

The family dinner table is the perfect place to define limits of acceptable behavior and acceptable conversation. Earlier in this chapter you read about ways to make conversation interesting and fun. This discussion has to do with conversations that are off limits at the dinner table.

Body parts and functions are not suitable topics of conversation when eating. Vivid descriptions of gory movies, accidents and illnesses aren't either. These topics can cause sensitive diners to lose their appetites quickly.

Older children should know better; younger ones need to be told. If they don't understand why not, since the discussion is not bothering *them* at all, you need to explain that these are conversations best saved for another time because they can make some people feel unwell.

Other conversational limits have to do with kindness. If the dinner table becomes the place where negative comments are made about specific individuals or about groups of people, children learn that these are acceptable feelings and acceptable things to say. Group criticism can breed discontent and even hate. Don't allow this to happen at your table. Instead, when a family member is feeling hostile about someone else, arrange to talk about it privately, one-on-one, after dinner.

Being There

Excusing family members from dinner is fine, some of the time. A last-minute invitation to someone else's house can be accepted by a child, with your approval; a telephone call asking permission to stay later at the mall may be approved; an extended sports or play practice can be understood. Constant absence, however, needs to be discussed, particularly if you are lenient when spontaneous requests occur. As discussed at the beginning of this chapter, the dinner table is often the only place the entire family gathers at one time with any regularity. Dwindling attendance on a daily basis is cause for a new look at priorities.

If making mealtime memorable at home is as important to you as it is to me, you have to share these feelings with your family members who aren't respecting that priority and reach an agreement. Sadly, if you do not, you will lose this opportunity for gathering together and sharing and for establishing traditions that often go on for generations.

Understanding also needs to be reached when older children return home to live after being independent for several years. It may be annoying to them to have to abide by the rules of the house, as used to total personal freedom as they may be, but it is equally annoying to you to constantly be purchasing quantities of food with the expectation that they will be present at mealtime. There usually are many readjustment problems to work out with those who are returning to the nest; the greatest ones seem to focus around food and meals.

A frank discussion of your expectations and theirs should clear the air. Clear communication solves many problems. Whether the solution is that you will expect them for dinner unless you hear from them to the contrary, with ample notice, or that they will be responsible for their own meals (from shopping to cooking to clean-up), it will give you all a common ground to smooth the way to comfortable communal living.

THE TELEPHONE

As mentioned earlier, the telephone should not be allowed to intrude on your dinner time unless it is of urgency or from another country where it would be difficult for you to call back. When you receive a call, say, "Ellie, we're just starting dinner—

may I call you back in about forty-five minutes?" This precedent shows children how to disconnect politely and quickly from a call.

Some families do not answer their telephone during dinner, letting the answering machine take a message. In other households, whoever answers says, "She's at dinner right now, may she call you back?" These are all fine alternatives, but I see nothing wrong with permitting the person being called to deliver his or her own message, even if it is slightly disruptive.

RESPECTING ELDERS

We have something to relearn from Oriental cultures when it comes to respecting elders. Parents have forgotten how to expect it *from* their children, and often have neglected to teach it *to* their children. There are a few simple rules of respect that all children should practice with their parents, and certainly with all guests and visitors to their home. A young person (boy or girl) should:

- Stand the first time an adult guest (male or female) enters the room. This should be automatic and should be accompanied by a greeting, such as, "Hello, Mrs. Barrett." Once is enough—there is no need to bounce up and down every time Mrs. Barrett comes into the room again.

- Remain standing at the table until the adults are seated; children should never be the first to sit down unless told to do so.

- Wait to begin eating until the hostess has begun or until she has suggested that her guests start.

- Assume responsibility as a host, offering refreshment, a seat or whatever to any guest. (This courtesy is extended to peers and younger children as well as to adults.)

BEFORE AND AFTER

Unity can be achieved in small ways before and after dinner, as well as during. Assigning responsibilities builds a sense of responsibility. It also gives parent and child or siblings a time to work together. Up to a certain age, usually about eleven, children want to help. They should be encouraged to do so, even if it takes you a little more time. Teaching skills then leads to better help later!

Do make sure that pot handles are not extended over the edge of the stove, that any chopping and cutting is done with a manageable knife and that candle-lighting is closely supervised and matchbook safety is discussed.

If table-setting is an assigned task, talk about where forks, spoons and knives go. If dish-washing is a participatory project, remind the washer about the backs of plates and dishes and the undersides of pots and pans.

All these details are part of what goes into making mealtime a pleasurable experience—not just the end result.

PRACTICE MAKES PERFECT

If it is at all possible to do so, even once a year, take your children to a formal sit-down restaurant so they can be proud of their manners and all they have learned. Although fast food restaurants are worthy of good manners, too, they do not provide opportunity for all the skills your children have learned.

Before you go, talk about courtesy to servers, how to request something, the function of a maitre d', and how to read a menu. *(See Chapter Five for restaurant manners.)*

THE CHILDREN'S TABLE

Many large families, when aunts and uncles and cousins get together for a meal, automatically set a "children's table." The philosophy seems to be that conversation is easier if the younger ones are off by themselves, usually in another room, that the "adult table" stays neater and that the children will do fine fending for themselves.

I do not mean to sound critical of this practice, but I do suggest instead, if more than one table is set, that adults and children intermingle at both. Thinking that young cousins who see one another rarely will fall into easy conversation and be able to overcome long silences may be overly optimistic. Shunting the children aside sends a message that they are rather a nuisance and that they wouldn't possibly know how to behave among adult company.

The argument I have heard in favor of children's tables comes from adults who have never had to sit at one. The argument against is raised by adults who did and who have never forgotten how they felt—that the experience was not fun at all.

Gatherings of family and friends should be safe and comfortable environments for children to practice their manners and to enjoy the fun of family get-togethers. If they are denied these extra chances to participate in memorable mealtimes, I feel they are denied a little bit of their heritage, as well. These are some of the occasions on which traditions are built, where special recipes are served and where stories of the past as well as the present are told. Because the dinner table brings an intimacy to any gathering—more so than when everyone is sitting in the yard and talking or standing in the living room having many small-group conversations—I believe its magic moments should be shared with children.

Manners serve to make family mealtime positive, gracious, calm and focused so that the most important values inherent are those of mutual respect and the nurturing of a sense of self-worth among all who are gathered. When the family shares meals together with no distractions, and affection sets the mood, children learn and grow in emotional stability and personal well-being. They receive care and love in an environment that enables them to give both back. They will take these values with them wherever they go, and someday pass them on, along with the traditions you have built together, to their own families.

2

Entertaining with Finesse:

From Barbecues to Banquets

There are many ingredients which, mixed together, produce close to perfect hosts and hostesses. In more or less an equal ratio, they include organization, a genuine sense of hospitality, enthusiasm, interest, creativity, sensitivity and foresight.

None of these is a magic ingredient, although it may seem that some people are more perfect hosts than others by virtue of magic. Rather, each is a learned ability, with some innate skill stirred in. The latter can come with practice; one does not have to be born with it.

Perhaps the best possible table manners and party advice for any host centers around one thought: *Don't hold your guests hostage.* Don't invite guests for dinner at eight and not serve until eleven. Don't invite guests to a birthday party and not light the candles on the cake until the latest possible hour. Don't pour coffee an hour after dessert is over, dragging the meal on interminably.

This doesn't mean that a dinner party or a birthday party or any other kind of entertainment must be rushed. It does mean that organizing your party well enables you to provide the purpose of your invitation, such as dinner, in a timely fashion within an hour of when you have invited guests to arrive. This allows for an ample cocktail hour and a leisurely dinner, *after* which you hope guests will choose to remain to visit and enjoy themselves. If they must leave, they are free to do so after a reasonable period of time (approximately one hour) without rudeness, for your main entertainment is completed.

If you invite them to arrive at seven and a two and one-half hour cocktail "hour" ensues, several things happen. Guests usually have too much to drink. Guests begin to look at their watches in anxiety. Guests must call the babysitter and say they are going to be later than expected. Guests ultimately must eat and run. They can't leave before dessert and coffee are served, for this would seem rude to you. But by serving them late, you are forcing them to stay longer than they might have otherwise—certainly longer than they thought they would—and you are trapping them or holding them hostage in your house. You want your parties to be events people look forward to attending, not ordeals to which they consider bringing their sleeping bags and pillows.

This chapter deals mainly with the requirements for the sort of at-home dinner with which most of us are familiar and which we enjoy. By taking the suggestions that appeal to you, by eliminating the details that would be difficult for you or which seem unnatural to you, and by combining the elements that are suitable to your home and your friends, you can use the information as it should be used—as a guide. Remember always, it is far less important to have matching silver or delicate crystal than it is to be a warm, relaxed and gracious party-giver. Self-confidence helps you to be all these things, and a knowledge that you are doing things correctly—to the very best of your ability—gives you the assurance to entertain easily and well.

Whether your dinner party guests number eight or one

hundred, the requisites for a successful party are the same. They are:

- *Guests* who are congenial.
- *A menu* that is well planned and suited to your guests' tastes.
- *An attractive table* with everything in perfect condition: linen pressed, silver polished, glassware sparkling.
- *Food* that is well prepared.
- *Servants* (if you have them or are hiring for the evening) who are competent and pleasant.
- *A gracious and cordial hostess and host* who are welcoming and at the same time enjoy their guests.

MAKING YOUR GUESTS COMFORTABLE

If the reason behind to any entertaining you do is that you want to please your guests in a personal way, you will succeed, whether the entertainment is a quiet cup of tea for the two of you or a lavish gala for a multitude.

To make your guests comfortable, you must be comfortable yourself. If the thought of providing dinner for twelve gives you hives but entertaining five other people is easy and fun for you, don't invite eleven. If a formal dinner party is something you enjoy giving but organizing a barbecue is beyond you, forget barbecues. There are as many formulas for entertaining as there are personalities. In entertaining as in life, concentrate on doing well what you do best and your entertaining occasions will be successful.

Who, What, When, Where and Why

The first considerations when you entertain at home are those of *where* and *what*. They are the space you have available for entertaining and the degree of formality you want and can achieve within that space. Someone who lives in a small house that has a large deck or patio would be more comfortable inviting guests to a barbecue or backyard picnic than to a formal dinner, while someone who has rooms with generous proportions could more easily give a formal dinner party.

No matter what your available space is, part of the same consideration is what type of party you can give comfortably and how many guests you can accommodate. Comfortably means being so organized that you spend the majority of your time with your guests, not in the kitchen. To do this, you must prepare as much as possible in advance and plan a menu that enables you to serve as the host or hostess, not as the cook or waiter or waitress.

Eight is usually the maximum number that you can serve yourself at a sit-down dinner. You can certainly cook for as many guests as you want and invite them to a buffet dinner, but to serve a seated dinner of more than eight efficiently and quickly it is almost essential to have an assistant. For more than sixteen the services of two people are recommended—one to help at the bar, pass hors d'oeuvres and serve dinner, the other to work in the kitchen. Greater numbers, of course, require more help.

The composition of your guests, or the *who* part of your planning, is an equally important consideration. You certainly do not want to have to carry the conversation throughout your party; you want people to find each other interesting and to be able to talk to each other without your constant guidance. With this in mind, it is wise to think about common interests among guests who are not already acquainted with one another. When your party is comprised of people who already know one another, you want to be sure that they still are getting along and are continuing to enjoy one another's company. It is not your role to reunite the Hatfields and the McCoys at your party. One of my friends says she would not dream of having a party without her brother and sister-in-law in attendance, for she can always count on them to be gregarious, entertaining, charming and witty. Every good party needs at least one of these important hostess helpers!

The lasting memories from your well-planned gathering should be those of camaraderie, laughter, comfort and the melding of tastes—the tastes that you provide at your table and the taste with which your environment is planned.

The *when* of your party-planning has everything to do with the *what*. There are ways to gather people together any time of the day or night, guided by your interest in providing appropriate refreshment. "When" can be brunch at noon or after-the-ball breakfast at 2 A.M. or any time in between. It can be a picnic at the beach at dusk, a strawberry fest on a spring afternoon, or a traditionally formal dinner at eight.

As long as your *what* and *when* are reasonably matched, your guests will know what to expect. When you invite guests to a luncheon party at 2 P.M., however, without specifying that lunch will be served, they will not expect it and will probably eat before they arrive. When you invite people to a party which begins at 8 P.M. but don't mention dinner in the invitation, they probably will not expect to be fed a full meal but rather will expect after-dinner drinks and snacks. Be specific, particularly if your "when" is at an unusual hour for what you are serving.

The *why* of your entertainment can be any reason at all—to view the first appearance of your night-blooming cereus; to celebrate a promotion; to rejoice that spring has arrived yet again; or just because.

As family meals are often the only time members of one household have a chance to be together in one place at one time, focused on one another, so are meal-based get-togethers with friends often the only time people who care about one another have the opportunity to share thoughts and catch up on each other's lives.

Intimate meals with friends provide the opportunity for good conversation without interruption in a way that card parties, going to the movies, or large gatherings do not. The desire to have this time together is reason enough to do so.

Setting the Tone

Flowers, music, seating arrangements, sunshine, candle-light—these are all things that will create the ambience for your party. Study the rooms you will use. Eliminate clutter, newspapers, pet hair, dead or drooping flowers, dust and all the other things that will detract from your ambience.

Flowers needn't be arranged in elaborate containers. A bunch of daffodils in a pretty pottery pitcher sets the tone for a casual brunch. Two sprays of orchids in a thin, fluted vase add elegance to a formal table. Match color, mood and your own artistry in adding touches of color and freshness to your environment.

Music can help establish the mood, and keep it going. It is particularly important at the beginning, when just a few people have gathered and conversation is just getting started. It fills brief silences and it relaxes—as long as what you have chosen to play is neither overwhelming nor intrusive.

The Beginning

One of the most important times to exert your energy when entertaining is at the beginning of the party. This is the time when people are the most uncertain—have they come too early or too late, what should they do with their handbags or coats, how do they best hand you the bottle of wine they have brought, do they know a single other soul to talk to—and you are the least focused, running through your mental checklist and being a little nervous yourself. If the doorbell keeps ringing and you must greet each guest, you naturally are leaving the one who just arrived to his own devices. It is always interesting to watch children at the beginning of a birthday party—as the first child is dropped off, he climbs out of the car, hands over his gift, and stands with the birthday child. When the next car arrives, both children run to greet the new arrival, and soon a veritable horde is running to welcome each new guest. In between, they run back to the middle of the yard or living room, but they never leave one another. I think that most adults would do this, too, if they could. It is much more comfortable to be part of that welcoming group than it is to stand alone!

With this in mind, the thoughtful host or hostess makes sure that early arrivals, in particular, are given extra attention, or a job to do, or a tour, or a drink, or a seat (as long as you sit with them). Since there are always last-minute things to do before a party of any sort, one of the ways to make a guest feel comfortable fast is to keep him with you, giving him a task, or project of a few minutes' duration. If you are still working in the kitchen, take him to the kitchen with you, offer him a drink and ask him to put crackers in a basket. The very warmth and ambience of the kitchen, combined with your company and the feeling of being useful, will put any guest who thinks he has erred by being too prompt right at ease. As more guests arrive, they will probably gravitate to the kitchen, too, so that by the time you move them all to the patio or the living room or wherever you would prefer them to be, they are feeling quite at home and have lost any awkwardness and uncertainty.

It is incumbent upon you to stay with them, as they settle in to the mood of your party. Any meal that requires more than fifteen minutes of preparation time after your guests have arrived is not the right meal. You are not the hired chef and waitress, you are the hostess, and your skills as hostess, or host, are necessary to the success of your party. If you are absent, your guests are going to wonder why you invited them in the first place, since it is obvious that it was not to enjoy their company. Don't leave guests on their own, do introduce strangers and initiate their conversation, do smile and set a tone of graciousness and happiness, and your guests will have a good time. Any party started with friendliness and warmth is a good party.

The End

Right here, before we even talk about the how-to's of your entertainments, it must be said that one of the worst mistakes a hostess can make is to bury herself in the kitchen after dinner, scraping plates, clattering flatware, loading the dishwasher. Nothing says "the end" faster. Guests feel you are signaling that you want them to leave; or they feel they must help. There will always be dishes to do; this particular party, this gathering of friends at this moment in time, will not always be there. Part of your party planning includes leaving the clean up until later, *after* everyone has gone home.

GREETING GUESTS

At very large formal dinners guests are greeted at the door by a servant who takes their coats. The hostess stands in the living room, near the door. As guests enter she greets them with a smile and a handshake and welcomes them. She may simply say, "I'm very glad to see you," or "I'm so glad that you could come!" but her smile is full of warmth. The host, who is circulating and talking to other guests, excuses himself and comes to greet newcomers as soon as he can.

Most dinners, however, are much less formal. The host and hostess stay near the door if possible, or if they happen to be in the living room, they go together to greet their guests when the doorbell rings. If the host is serving cocktails he brings them what they wish, or he sees that the waiter or bartender takes their order. The hostess introduces them to people they do not know.

If cocktails are served, dinner should be planned for approximately one hour later than the time on the invitation; twenty minutes later if drinks are not served, to allow late arrivals a moment of relaxation. During this period the hostess may slip out to the kitchen to attend to last-minute details or to be sure that her helpers are having no problems.

THE LATE GUEST

Fifteen minutes is the established length of time that a hostess need delay her dinner for a late guest. To wait more than twenty minutes, at the outside, would be showing rudeness to many for the sake of one. When the late guest finally enters the dining room he must go up to the hostess and apologize for being late.

The hostess should not express anger or take the guest to task, but should say something polite such as, "I'm so sorry you had such a bad drive but I was sure you wouldn't want us to wait dinner." The latecomer is served whatever course is being eaten at the time he arrives. Of course, if that happens to be dessert the hostess should serve him the entrée first.

PARTIES WITH HELP

Almost any dinner where guests are seated at a table and are served by someone other than themselves is considered a "formal" dinner today. Of course there are all degrees of formality, depending upon the dress, the table setting, the food served, and the type of service. Emily Post wrote in 1922 that "it is not possible to give a formal dinner without the help of servants." Yet today the hostess who cooks a perfectly prepared meal and serves it at a beautifully set table is considered to have given a "formal" dinner, with nary a servant in sight.

If you do have servants or elect to hire help for a party, utilizing their skills well is important.

Serving Staff

If you have live-in help, they will presumably have learned to serve in the way you like best. Most of us, however, must hire temporary help for the evening when we want to entertain more than eight guests formally. Catering services and specialized employment agencies are resources for temporary help. Although they may be professionals at what they do, you still need to give them instructions so that they are able to assist according to your wishes. Temporary help is generally hired to cook and/or serve and clean up. Unless the help has been hired to do otherwise, it is up to the hostess to do all the other preparation, from setting the table and arranging flowers to making sure the bar is stocked and there is plenty of ice.

The method of paying temporary help varies in different localities and also depends on the policy of the agency. Some caterers send a bill for their services and prefer that you do not add a tip. Others send a bill indicating that you may add a tip. If the help has been hired from an employment agency or by you personally, you simply pay them before they leave at the rate you have agreed upon, adding the appropriate tip. In any case, it is most important to establish the method and amount of payment at the time servants are hired to avoid embarrassment or unpleasantness later.

Catering Service/Cook

A catering service will provide all the elements of the meal with instructions as to how they are to be heated, etc., or it will provide the food and a cook. If there is to be a cook, he or she arrives early enough to learn the workings of the kitchen and to have time for preparation of the meal.

If there is no cook, the food is either picked up or delivered early enough for the hostess to add whatever finishing touches are needed.

Many catering services also provide bartenders and waiters/waitresses, if required.

Bartender

When cocktails are to be served to a sizeable group, a bartender arrives early enough to set up the bar, see that he or she has all the necessary ingredients, and be ready when the first guest arrives. It is a good idea, when hiring a bartender, to run through a checklist first as to what he or she needs, from orange slices to seltzer to how much ice to how many bottles of white wine. An experienced bartender will be able to provide excellent guidance as to quantity so you can be prepared for all requests.

Waiters/Waitresses

Temporary waiters and waitresses can provide many services. These should be discussed at the time hiring arrangements are made. Hired helpers may wait in the hall to direct guests, take coats, etc., they may pass hors d'oeuvres, assist the bartender in passing drinks if guests do not go to the bar themselves, and they serve at the table. They also may be expected to clean up. Depending on their duties, they arrive early enough to perform whatever their first function will be.

The bartender and waitress ordinarily do not leave until the guests have been ushered out, the last glass washed, and the last ashtray emptied. However, if they are hired on an hourly basis, the hostess may specify ahead of time that they may leave at ten or eleven, or whenever she wishes. The cook, however, unless all three work as a unit, leaves as soon as the cooking utensils and dinner service have been washed and the kitchen made immaculate.

PARTIES WITHOUT HELP

When there is no extra help at a dinner party, the host and/or hostess see to their guests needs directly. They pass trays of hors d'oeuvres once or twice, sometimes with the help of a close friend. Hors d'oeuvres are then left in an accessible spot and guests help themselves. Trays or dishes are removed as they are emptied.

Guests are offered a drink when they arrive and may be asked to help themselves after the first drink is prepared by the host.

If there are only a few guests, the host may hang their coats in a hall closet. If there are more wraps than a closet can conveniently hold, guests are asked to put them in a bedroom or other room that won't be used for the party.

WHEN DINNER IS ANNOUNCED

When dinner is ready to be served, the candles are lighted and water glasses are filled. If there is no help, the first course, if it is not a hot course, is in place so that the hostess may sit down right away with her guests. The hostess announces to the group, "Dinner is ready, shall we go in?" if the group is small. If the group is large, she may ask two or three good friends to help her in moving the other guests toward the dining room so that she doesn't need to stand in the doorway and shout. If she is having difficulty getting people to respond, she may, if she wishes, suggest that her guests bring their cocktails to the table to encourage them to delay no longer just to finish their drinks.

At a very formal dinner when the table is being made ready by servants and there is a butler, the butler approaches the hostess to tell her that dinner is ready, and she then asks her guests to move to the dining room. Again, the first course, if not a hot course, may be in place. If it is a hot course, such as soup, the butler serves it after people are seated.

The host leads the way in to dinner with the female guest of honor whom he seats on his right. Other guests walk in with whomever they are talking to when dinner is announced. The hostess is always the last to go into the dining room when place cards are used. If there are no place cards, she goes ahead to tell guests where to sit. Women sit down as soon as they find their places, even though the hostess remains standing until everyone is at his chair. The men hold the chairs for the women on their right. The men do not sit down until the hostess is seated. The male guest of honor, even though he has escorted the hostess in, seats the lady on his right, and the man on the hostess's left seats her.

When a single woman entertains at a large dinner, she seats the woman of honor, if there is one, at one end of the table and herself at the other end. If a man is acting as host, he is seated to the woman of honor's left. The man of honor is seated to the hostess's right, and other guests are seated alternating men and women around the table.

The Order of Service

Whether there is serving help or not, the lady of honor on the host's right is always served each dish first. If there is serving help, servers move around the table counterclockwise, serving the host last. The hostess is never served first. *(The diagrams in Chapter Three explain seating and service arrangements.)*

When there is no serving help and the host or hostess fill plates and pass them, they say "This is for you" when giving the first plate to the guest of honor so she knows she is to keep it and not pass it down the table. The second plate is passed down the table on the right side to whoever is sitting at the opposite end from the host. The rest of the guests are served in order, working back toward the guest of honor. The process is then repeated on the host's left side. He serves himself last.

When food is served directly from the kitchen, service is also counterclockwise with the host served last. Plates are served from the guest's left side and removed, if possible, from the right.

Since any of these procedures can take considerable time and the food will surely be getting cold, it is important that the host or hostess ask the guests to start after three or four people have been served. If the host and hostess forget to do so, one of the guests is perfectly correct in beginning to eat.

Clearing the Table

Dishes are removed two at a time. They are never stacked or scraped at the table. Each time something is taken to the kitchen, you may bring back dessert plates, salad and salad plates, or whatever is needed. If you wish, you may put a dessert plate at each place you have cleared as you return to take the next plate. Or as soon as you have removed the host's plate, you may put a stack of dessert plates and the dessert in front of him, and he may serve it while you are finishing the table-clearing.

If finger bowls are used, they may be brought in on plates after dessert is served or they may be placed on a small doily along with the dessert fork and spoon on the dessert plate. The diner puts the finger bowl, lifted with the doily, above his plate, and the fork and spoon each to its proper side. If no finger bowls are used, dessert may be brought in from the kitchen already on the plates and placed before the guests in the same order as was the main course. In other words, any system that speeds and smooths the changing of courses is acceptable, so that your guests do not feel that you are going to too much trouble. To guests who offer to help you clear, you must say, "No, thank you, really it is easier to do it myself," or you will find that everyone but one or two of your guests is suddenly on his or her feet and in the kitchen. Of course, a very close friend or relative may be asked in advance to help, and a son or daughter should be expected to help, but your other guests should be just that— guests—and remain at the table.

After-Dinner Coffee and Drinks

See pages 103–105 for the serving of after dinner coffee and drinks.

The Courses for Dinner

Six courses are the maximum for even the most elaborate formal dinner. They are:

1) Soup *or* fresh fruit cup *or* melon *or* shellfish (clams, oysters or shrimp)

2) Fish course (*or* on rare occasions, a dish such as sweetbreads instead of fish and omitted if shellfish is served first)

3) The entrée, or main course

4) Salad

5) Dessert

6) Coffee

Notice that the salad is served between the entrée and dessert. This is correct in spite of the custom in almost all restaurants of serving it as a first course. Unless you know that a group of friends at a causal dinner prefer it first, salad should be served as stated here, or it may be served with the entrée on a separate salad plate.

One should always try to choose a well-balanced menu; an especially rich dish is balanced by a simple one. Coquilles St. Jacques (scallops with a thick cream sauce) might perhaps be followed by medallions of lamb, Cornish game hens or a filet mignon; broiled fish by a more elaborate meat dish.

Consider the appearance of the food that you serve. Avoid a dinner of white sauces from beginning to end: creamed soup, creamed sweetbreads, followed by breast of chicken and mashed potatoes. Combine flavors intelligently. Don't serve all sweet dishes: beet soup, duck basted with currant jelly, a fruit salad, and a sugary dessert. In these examples, each dish is good in itself but unappetizing in the monotony of its combination.

Wine

Tradition has always decreed that one particular wine goes with one particular food, but unless the meal is strictly formal there is no reason why the host may not choose any wine he thinks his guests would like. The two most important considerations in choosing a wine are not the cost or where it came from, but that it complements the food with which it is served and pleases the palates of the people drinking it.

Wine glasses are filled only halfway, never to the top of the glass. If more than one variety of wine is to be served during dinner, there should be a glass for each wine.

Wine glasses should be picked up by the stem rather than the bowl. In the case of white wine and champagne this helps to keep the wine cool, and in the case of all wines, including red wines, it enables you to appreciate the color.

There are five main categories of wine we should consider.

APERITIFS

Aperitifs include Lillet, Dubonnet, Campari, Cinzano, dry or sweet vermouths and sherry. They are generally served as a before-meal drink, but sherry may be the first wine offered at dinner and also is served at lunch or supper. It is usually offered with a soup that contains sherry. It should not be offered with cream of chicken soup or vichyssoise, but it would be an appropriate accompaniment to black bean or green turtle soup. Sherry should be put in a decanter at room temperature and poured into small, V-shaped glasses. If you don't have sherry glasses, small wine glasses or liqueur glasses are suitable substitutes. Sherry can stand being decanted almost indefinitely without spoiling.

Other aperitifs are served according to preference, either in a small, low-ball glass with ice, or chilled or at room temperature in a small aperitif glass.

WHITE WINE

White wines include Chablis, Meursault, Burgundy, Montrachet, Muscadet Chardonnay, Sauvignon Blanc, Chenin Blanc, Sancerre, Pinot Grigio, Gavi and Reisling. Dry white wines should be served chilled. They may be chilled in the refrigerator for several hours or even days before being used, or may be cooled in a bucket or cooler filled with a mixture of ice and cold water. The actual melting of the ice in the water will cool the wine faster than if it is immersed in cracked ice alone. Drawing the cork and turning the bottle from time to time will hasten the cooling.

Traditionally, white wines are served with "white" meats such as fish, chicken, and veal, and with fruit and salads. This is still the case, but many people drink white wine as their cocktail choice and prefer to continue drinking it throughout the meal, no matter what the entrée is.

RED WINE

Red wines, for the most part, are served at a cool room temperature. If they are too cool, they may be warmed by placing the hands around the bowl of the glass, or by being left before serving in a warm spot (but never over a burner or flame). The major categories include Bordeaux, Beaujolais, Burgundy, Chianti, Rioja, Cabernet Sauvignon, Pinot Noir and Zinfandel.

Traditionally, red wines are served with beef, certain cheese dishes, pasta with a red sauce and some game birds, although, as with white wine, red wines are often drunk regardless of the entrée as a wine of preference or because they have been drunk during the cocktail hour before dinner. This would be more likely with a claret, a light red wine, than with a burgundy, which is much heavier.

The procedure for serving a fine vintage red wine is somewhat complicated but should be followed carefully if its excellence is to be appreciated. A day or two before it is to be used, the wine should be removed from the wine cellar or closet. This is done by transferring the bottle into a straw basket as gently as possible, maintaining the bottle in a semihorizontal position. Actually in the basket it should be tilted 15 or 20 degrees more toward the vertical than it was in the bin, and it is left in this position for a day at least to permit any disturbed sediment to settle.

If you do not have a wine cellar, purchase the wine several days before your dinner and follow the same procedure. The bottle should be opened an hour or so before serving. At this time, the foil is neatly cut away to prevent the wine from coming in contact with it while being poured. For the same reason a damp cloth is used to wipe the mouth of the bottle, removing any accumulated dirt and grime. The cork is then carefully pulled and placed beside the neck of the bottle in its basket in order that the host or any interested guest may note that it is undamaged. During this hour the bottle is open, the wine is given an opportunity to "breathe" and rid itself of any musty or other unpleasant odor it might have absorbed in the cellar.

It should be served in the basket, with the label showing to permit each guest to note what he is being offered. Caution must be taken when pouring the wine to avoid any "backlash" or bubbling that can result if it is handled carelessly. This would agitate the sediment, which should be resting in the bottom of the bottle. Finally, it is obvious that the last inch or so should not be poured from the bottle, since this will be murky with sediment.

When a bottle of red wine is so heavy with sediment that the procedure given above will not result in a palatable drink, it may be decanted. Be sure that decanters you use are lead-free. Recent studies have found that many cut glass decanters, especially older and antique bottles, contain lead, which leaches into the contents of the decanter.

Rosé wines of the non-sparkling variety are in the red wine family. They are served somewhat chilled, generally with lighter entrées such as fish, veal, some chicken dishes and fruit.

SPARKLING WINES

This category of wine includes sparkling rosé, Zinfandel, sparkling burgundies, and sparkling white wines, including champagne.

Champagne is, above all other beverages, a sign of a very special dinner party. When other wines are included, it is served with the meat course, but when it is the only wine it is served as soon as the first course has begun. Its proper temperature depends upon its quality, but it is always chilled.

Champagne, like white wine, is put in the refrigerator for a day and then chilled further by putting it into a cooler with a little water as well as ice. Occasionally, holding the bottle by the neck, turn it back and forth a few times. Also, when opening, be sure to wrap the bottle in a towel or napkin as a protection in case it explodes.

DESSERT WINES

Sweet sherry, port, and Madeira wines often accompany a dessert course. They are served at room temperature, with the exception of Sauternes, which are served chilled in white wine glasses, and are poured from a decanter after dessert is served.

(See pages 86–89 for the shapes and sizes of wine glasses and page 92 for the placement of glasses on the table.)

BUFFET DINNERS

There are three great advantages to a buffet dinner that appeal to all of us. First, you can accommodate many more guests than your dining-room table will seat. It is important, however, to restrict the number so that there will be places for everyone to sit down, and also so that there will be room for the guests to move about freely when serving themselves. Be sure that there are enough seats for everyone. *Never* assume that guests enjoy standing up and eating, perching on the arm of a chair, balancing on the stairway, or sitting on the floor. In fact, the older your guests, the less they will like that type of seating.

Second, lack of service is no handicap. Because a buffet is truly a "do-it-yourself" party, even the hostess without help may spend almost the entire evening with her guests.

And third, it has the informality that most of us so much enjoy. There is something about sitting in one place before dinner, going into the dining room to help yourself, then coming back to the same place or finding a new place, as you prefer, that makes buffet parties so popular. Also you are free to choose your dinner companions yourself, as you cannot do at a seated dinner.

When dinner is ready, it is announced by the hostess and people in more or less of a queue file around the buffet table. The guests go first, urged by the hostess, if necessary, but whether it is a seated dinner or a buffet the hostess should *never* serve herself first.

If people continue to sit and wait to be served, the hostess has to encourage them a little, saying, "Please go into the dining room and help yourselves to dinner." If they linger at the buffet, carrying on a long conversation and blocking the table, she should suggest that they take their plates into the other room.

The only serving detail of importance in a buffet meal is the clearing away of used dishes. If the hostess has help for the evening, each plate is removed as soon as it is put down. Also, if there are servants, they refill the glasses of seated guests from time to time, and the main dishes may be passed for second helpings. The servantless hostess suggests to her guests that they go back for "a little more" and then she can ask close friends to help her take the used dishes to a convenient table or sideboard, from which she can take them to the kitchen as unobtrusively as possible.

Beverages may be set on a separate table from the food for guests to help themselves, or a tray of wine or iced tea or whatever may be passed by the host as guests are finding places to eat. Glasses are set on the tables at a seated buffet but they are not filled until guests are seated. In this case, the host goes from table to table and pours for each guest, or if a wine bottle or pitcher of another beverage is on each table, the person seated nearest would pour for those at the table.

The Menu

It does not matter what foods you choose as long as they are well prepared and easy to eat with fork alone if your guests are not seated at tables. Beyond that, merely use a reasonable amount of common sense in selecting dishes that will be satisfying to the people invited.

There are countless delicious menus to be tried; the only limit is your imagination. If you wish to be very elaborate, or if you have a great many guests, you may wish to serve two main dishes. If you do this, be sure both will be complemented by the same vegetables and condiments.

Other buffet menus may be very simple—a casserole, rice, a vegetable and salad; lasagna and a salad with hot Italian bread; sliced turkey, cranberry sauce, cornbread stuffing and a green vegetable—the combinations are endless but needn't be comprised of countless dishes.

Types of Buffet

REAL BUFFET

When guests at a real buffet have served themselves in the dining room, they simply take their plates into another room (at a large party, often several other rooms are used), hold their plates on their laps and set their glasses on the nearest table. Your guests will be much more comfortable and there will be much less chance of an accident if you set a small table (like a folding tray table) near each chair, or at least by each chair not within easy reach of a coffee or side table.

SEATED OR SEMI-BUFFET

At this type of buffet your guests may be seated at the dining table (if not being used as the buffet table) and at small tables—sturdy card tables, perhaps—in your living room, den, hall or wherever. This arrangement is, of course, dependent on your having large enough rooms so that the tables will not be in the way before dinner or while the guests are serving themselves. Tables are covered with cloths of almost any color and style, and the places are set as for any seated dinner.

COCKTAIL BUFFETS

A cross between a cocktail party and a buffet dinner party, the cocktail buffet is the choice of many for entertaining all except the smallest and most informal groups. Because there is usually enough food presented that the guests need not have dinner afterward and therefore are expected to linger longer, the invitation frequently states only the hour of arrival. In many sections of the country this is likely to be a little later than a simple cocktail party, often at six-thirty or seven. It should be made very clear that the gathering is a "cocktail buffet," so that the guests realize that they will be served some substantial food and need not make other plans for dinner.

The menu may vary from simple to very elaborate, but even the simplest menu must provide more than just hors d'oeuvres. The least that one can expect is a platter of cold meat—ham, chicken, or roast beef—slices of breads, accompanying dishes such as raw vegetables and possibly some small sandwiches. This minimum type of buffet may be eaten standing near the table without a plate. The meat can be placed on a slice of bread and eaten like a sandwich, and the raw vegetables picked up and dipped in a sauce.

For a more elaborate buffet you might include one or more hot dishes, generally casseroles that can be kept warm on a hot plate or served in a chafing dish over a low flame. In this case, of course, there must be stacks of plates and rows of forks. The main difference between this type of buffet and a buffet dinner is that only one real course is served, although cookies or cake may be offered with coffee.

If you do not wish to go into the added complication of plates and silver you may choose a hot dish such as bite-sized meatballs or frankfurters, tiny hot potatoes dipped in salt, and hot bread or rolls with a cheese fondue, all of which may be speared with a toothpick. Tacos are hearty and can be bought frozen. Fritonga, a South American mixture of fried bits of meat, banana slices, potatoes and popcorn, will give you a reputation for originality. Chicken wings dipped in batter and deep fried or simply broiled or baked in a sweet-and-sour sauce are delectable too. Use your imagination and you will delight your guests, but don't experiment on them—try out your new ideas on family or close friends beforehand.

LUNCHEONS

Social luncheons may be held in someone's home, or they may be held at a club or restaurant. The number of guests you can accommodate in your dining room or at small individual tables, as well as the amount of time you can spend on preparation and the help that is available to you, determines the choice of locale.

The Menu

The menu generally resembles that of a light dinner but would include no more than two or three courses. There are five possible courses to select from:

1) Fruit, or soup in cups

2) Eggs or shellfish

3) Fowl, meat (not a roast), fish, or a casserole containing one of these

4) Salad (a side salad to either 2. or 3., or an entrée salad, such as a club salad, a chef's salad, or a salad Niçoise

5) Dessert

Breads may be served with any course. Hot breads, such as croissants or biscuits, accompany many luncheon menus nicely, as do English muffins, dinner rolls, corn bread, or fruit muffins. They are passed as often as necessary. Butter is usually put on the butter plate beforehand, and it is passed again, whenever necessary, until the table is cleared for dessert.

Soup at a luncheon is never served in soup plates, but in two-handled cups. It is eaten with a teaspoon or a bouillon spoon, or after it has cooled sufficiently the cup may be picked up. It is almost always a clear soup, or a cold vichyssoise or gazpacho in the summer.

Beverages

Wine is often served with lunch. One wine is sufficient, and it should be a light one such as dry Rhine wine or a claret.

A chilled white wine with soda (a spritzer) may also be served in the summer, but iced tea or iced coffee is the usual choice. Tea is poured into the glasses and decorated with sprigs of fresh mint. Iced coffee should be passed around in a pitcher on a tray that also holds a bowl of granulated sugar, packets of artificial sweetener and a pitcher of cream. The guests pour their own coffee into tall glasses that are half full of ice and accompanied by long-handled spoons. Or if your luncheon is a buffet, a pitcher of each should be available close to the buffet table. A bowl of fruit punch may take the place of iced tea or coffee and appears cool and refreshing if it is prepared with floating slices of orange and lemon and is surrounded by glasses or cups adorned with fresh sprigs of mint.

In the winter many hostesses like to have hot coffee or tea served with the meal instead of, or in addition to, serving it later.

A pitcher of iced water is welcome in hot weather or glasses of water may already be on the table if it is a seated luncheon.

The Table

A lunch table may be the dining room table, several card tables, or a patio table for an al fresco luncheon. Depending on the formality of the luncheon, the table may be set with a tablecloth or with place mats. *(See pages 70–74 for table-setting suggestions.)*

TEAS

Afternoon teas have become increasingly popular over the past few years and are given just because they are fun; or in honor of visiting celebrities or new neighbors; to "warm" a new house; or for a houseguest. Invitations to an informal tea are almost always issued by telephone. However, if the occasion is more formal, the invitation is sent on a fill-in card or on your notepaper.

Tea-Party Guests

When a tea is given for someone, or to celebrate something special, it is, to some extent, "formal." Women wear dresses or suits, men wear suits and ties.

When there is a guest of honor, you introduce him or her to your other guests as they arrive. But rather than forming a receiving line, you and the guest of honor stand together near the door and talk for a little while with the arriving guests.

Otherwise, behavior is very informal. As a guest you may (and should) talk to anyone there, whether you have been introduced or not. You may return to the tea table as many times as you wish, but you may *not* overload your plate at any one time. When you are ready to leave (and you are not expected to stay until the very end at a large tea) you simply thank your host and hostess, say good-bye to the guest of honor and go.

The Menu

Food for a tea party is quite different from that served at a cocktail party. For one thing, much of the food is sweet—cookies, tarts, fruitcake or slices of iced cake are almost always offered. In addition, for those who do not have such a "sweet tooth," tea sandwiches are served. They are small, made on very thin bread and are usually cold, although in winter there is sometimes a tray of hot cheese puffs, pastry filled with mushrooms, etc. The sandwiches are light and delicate—watercress rolled in thin bread, a cherry tomato sliced on a round of bread, cream cheese on date-and-nut bread and crabmeat on toast are typical choices for tea-party menus.

Because nothing needs to be passed to the guests, it is perfectly possible for anyone to give a formal tea without help. If you have no maid, you set out the tray with everything except the boiling water before the guests arrive, leaving the kettle on the stove in the kitchen. Greet your guests at the door, tell them where to leave their coats, and when you are ready for tea simply fill the teapot from the kitchen kettle and carry it in to the tea table.

Making Good Tea

The most important part of the tea service is boiling water and plenty of it. To make good tea, first, half-fill the pot with boiling water, let it stand a moment or two to heat the teapot, and then pour it out. Put in a rounded teaspoonful of tea leaves or one tea bag for each cup. Half this amount may be used if the tea is of superb quality. Then pour on enough *actually boiling* water to cover the tea leaves about half an inch. It should steep at least five minutes (or for those who like it very strong, ten) before additional boiling water is poured on. When serving, pour half tea, half boiling water for those who like it weak. Increase the amount of tea for those who like it strong. The cup of *good* tea should be too strong without the addition of a little lively boiling water, which gives it freshness.

When tea has to stand a long time for many guests, the ideal way is to make a strong infusion in a big kettle on the kitchen stove. Let the tea actually boil three to four minutes on the range, then pour it through a sieve or filter into your hot teapot. The tea will not become bitter, and it does not matter if it gets quite cold. The boiling water poured over no more than the tablespoonful of such tea will make the drink hot enough.

Those Who Pour

Pouring is usually done by close friends of the party giver. Those close friends are asked beforehand if they will "do the honors," and unless they have a very valid reason not to, they should accept. Sometimes, after half an hour, the first two are relieved by two other friends.

Each person walks right up to the table and says, "May I have a cup of tea?"

The one pouring should smile and answer, "Certainly. How do you like it? Strong or weak? Would you like cream or lemon?" If the guest says, "Weak," boiling water is added, and according to the guest's wishes, sugar, cream or lemon. If the guest prefers coffee, he or she asks for it at the other end of the table. If you are not too busy pouring and the guest is alone, you make a few pleasant remarks, but if there are a number of people around the table waiting, you need only smile as you hand each guest a cup of tea or coffee.

COCKTAIL PARTIES

In many parts of the country cocktail parties have become the most common form of entertaining, and they can be the answer to a busy person's prayer. Along with open houses, barbecues, and picnics they provide a relatively simple answer to the rule that all invitations must be repaid. Their advantages over a dinner party are many in a society in which relatively few households have servants, and in which the cost of hiring temporary help or a caterer is beyond the reach of many. Cocktail parties require less preparation, they are less expensive than a dinner party, they are limited in time and you can entertain many more people at once in a small house. On the other hand, no one invited to a cocktail party feels as honored as if he had been invited to dinner, and at a large party the host and hostess cannot spend as much time with any one guest as they would if they were seated at a dinner table. Cocktail parties do provide an excellent opportunity for entertaining new acquaintances, particularly if you also wish to include the people at whose homes you met your new friends, and others to whom you want to introduce them.

Cocktail parties may be as large or small, as simple or elaborate, as you wish, and the ways of inviting people are varied. If the number of guests is small the invitation is almost always by telephone. For a larger party invitations are usually written on a printed fill-in card.

When there is to be no buffet, both the beginning and ending time is usually stated: "Cocktails from 5:00 to 7:00" rather than "Cocktails at 5:00."

At a cocktail party you may serve literally every sort of hors d'oeuvre or appetizer that you think tastes good and looks tempting—as long as it can be eaten with the fingers. At some cocktail parties small plates are placed on the hors d'oeuvres table and guests are expected to fill these plates with a variety of appetizers. This is all right if there are places for guests to take these plates and sit, putting their glasses down, to eat. This also helps keep the table freer—otherwise, guests tend to find a place around the hors d'oeuvres table where they stand and eat for a considerable time, one appetizer at a time, making it difficult for other guests to help themselves.

Two essential ingredients to a cocktail party are coasters and napkins, and plenty of both. The wise host places coasters on every surface all around the rooms that will be used during the party, to protect tabletops and other furniture. Napkins should be provided with drinks, as well as with any passed hors d'oeuvres, and should be placed on the hors d'oeuvres table, too.

At a large party, extra glasses are essential. Guests continually put down their glasses and forget which is theirs, or leave their empty ones behind when they go to the bar for another drink.

When planning bar purchases, as a general rule, figure that each guest will have at least three drinks. Since a quart of liquor will provide 21 one-and-a-half-ounce drinks, one bottle will serve approximately seven people.

Even though your party is called a cocktail party, not all of your guests may choose an alcoholic beverage, so you *must* have nonalcoholic drinks available. Tomato or other fruit juices, colas, mineral water and ginger ale all are popular substitutes. It is also thoughtful to have diet sodas available.

BYOB AND BYOF PARTIES

A group of friends may decide to get together informally with each providing something for the dinner. "BYO" means "Bring Your Own"—bottle or food, as the case may be. If the party is a "Bring Your Own Bottle" party, guests bring whatever they will be drinking. These bottles are not intended to be gifts for the host and hostess. They simply make it possible for the group to get together without anyone's incurring an enormous expense. Each person may initial his bottle, whether partly used or unopened, and take home any liquor that is left. The bottles are "pooled," however, at the party, and if someone runs out of Scotch, for example, he is offered some by one of the other Scotch-drinkers. A beer drinker may take a six-pack and offer extra cans to other beer drinkers.

Mixers and ice are provided by the host, who should also have soft drinks available. The host clears a table surface on which he places glasses, mixers and any drink additions, such as olives, lemon peel, orange slices, etc. Cocktail napkins and a container of stirrers should be on the table as well. Guests then mix their own drinks.

Bring-your-own-food or bring-a-dish parties are organized by the group and hosted by one person or couple who has the space and the inclination to provide it. The host and hostess who arrange this sort of evening are not "giving" the party— they are "organizing" it. There are several ways of doing this. The hostess may call several people and say, "Let's get a group together. We'll all bring one dish, and I'll have a keg of beer on hand." Or she may send written invitations asking each person to provide a specific dish. In this case, she would write "Come to a Pot-Luck Dinner" or a "Chip-in Dinner" at the top. Unless she has specified a dish *and* a bottle, she should provide the liquid refreshments. However she goes about it, the important thing is that she make it quite clear that she is not "giving" the entire party *before* the guest is trapped. It is inexcusable to receive someone's acceptance and then tell them they must bring a dish, or a bottle. The invitees must be free to refuse the invitation if they are unwilling or unable to contribute.

BARBECUES

A barbecue is an informal way to entertain just a few special friends or a large group, depending on your available space and your barbecue equipment. Ideally, two people host a barbecue, since one has to tend the grill while the other sees to bringing the other dishes from the kitchen. *(See pages 113–114 to learn about setting the barbecue table.)*

BRUNCHES

Brunch—a combination of breakfast and lunch that relies on both breakfast and lunch dishes for its menus, although it is held closer to the usual hour for lunch—is a pleasant sort of informal, even casual, way of entertaining. It is not unusual to find brunches being given on the day after a large party, especially if there are many out-of-town guests who have come for the "big" occasion. However, no such excuse is necessary if you find the late-morning hours convenient for you and your friends.

Informality is the rule for attire and attitude. Invitations may be telephoned. Menus include Bloody Marys, mimosas, other drinks from the bar and soft drinks, mineral waters and coffee and tea. Food is arranged on a buffet table less elaborately set than for lunch or dinner, but attractively and conveniently laid out. The menu can be casseroles, scrambled eggs with bacon and sausage, hot rolls, toast, sauteed potatoes, broiled tomatoes, waffles, creamed chicken or whatever you like to serve.

ENTERTAINING DILEMMAS

Every host eventually accrues a collection of stories about near-disasters, humorous moments, problems and solutions. While it is impossible to anticipate some of the odd things that can happen: a guest who gets his foot stuck in the dog's water dish and ruins his fine Italian leather shoe; the couple who chooses your house to stage a screaming match; the nightmare stereotype-come-true guest who puts your lampshade on her head; or your child suddenly needing to be rushed to the emergency room for stitches just as dinner is to be served, there are other things a host should be prepared to handle.

Inebriated Guests

The circumstances under which someone drinks too much, and how it becomes evident, are far too varied for the host or hostess to be able to deal with every eventuality. However, there are a few important steps to take when a guest becomes obnoxious or embarrassing at your party. First, if the offender becomes truly drunk, enlist the aid of the person or people he or she came with in getting the overindulger home or in helping should he or she be feeling ill. Of course, the drunken person may have come to the party alone. If it is a man, ask your husband or a male friend to help you deal with him. If it is a woman, deal with her yourself, unless you need someone's help in assisting or carrying her to a bedroom or a taxi. If the reveler is merely on the way to becoming loud, try to keep this guest from having any more to drink—to the point of saying you think perhaps he or she has had enough and asking, "How about a cup of coffee?" When a drunk becomes insulting or offensive, as sometimes happens, try to smooth it over with the victim, explaining that "Jim [or Joanne] has had a little too much to drink, and really doesn't know what he [or she] is saying." And get Jim or Joanne diverted, and away from the bar.

Most important, never let anyone who has had too much to drink get behind the wheel of a car. If there is no one to do the driving, you should see that a mutual friend sees him or her home safely, call a taxi or put him or her to bed in your home. For the safety of other travelers as well as his or her own, you must go to any lengths to prevent this person from driving. The fact that you would be legally liable for allowing this person to drive is incidental compared to your concern for everyone's safety.

Smokers

When you do not smoke or do not permit smoking in your house, you should provide an outdoor space, with chairs, for those who do. I find No Smoking signs posted in someone's home offensive, institutional and unnecessary and do not recommend their use. Some will say "the guest's comfort is paramount and if he smokes, you should get an ashtray," but I do not concur if it really bothers you or others. Smokers are so used to being unpopular today that a simple, "John, we promised the children there would be no smoking in the house," or "Cheryl, I'm going to have to show you to the smoking headquarters outside—Janie is allergic to smoke," when someone is about to light up or does light up inside, gives your message politely and inoffensively. Of course, this is more pleasant for the smoker in warm weather, but someone who really needs to have a cigarette will gladly put on his coat and stand in the coldest of snow storms just to do so.

Verbal Abusers

When someone at your party becomes offensive to you or another guest, you may feel free to ask him to leave. Your responsibility is to all your guests, and one among them who has become uncivilized and who does not see the error of his ways and apologize immediately does not belong there anymore. This is not an easy thing to do, but you should attempt to get him away from the group, explain that he is ruining your party and frightening others, and you would appreciate his staying in another room to "cool off," or leaving, whichever he prefers. Naturally, when someone becomes violent and out of control, you may have to call the police. This is not a pleasant thing to anticipate, but everyone's safety is what is important.

Inappropriateness

When a guest is telling vulgar jokes or making racist or other unpleasant remarks, you as host must tell him to stop. You can do this in as friendly a manner as possible, but his embarrassing lack of taste is an embarrassment to you, too, and must be curtailed quickly.

Pets on Premise

Your little Fifi may be the most adorable dog you have ever seen, but even if you have carefully trained her to hop in circles around the dinner table, she doesn't belong there when you are entertaining. She must be banned to the bedroom if she is going to beg, jump up, put her nose in guests' laps, bark, scratch or commit other doglike actions during your party. Even the most well-behaved dog is probably safer when not underfoot. You may be used to stepping over her, but your guests won't be and the risk of her being trampled or of a guest taking a serious spill after tripping on her isn't worth her being present.

Cats have a tendancy to investigate tabletops. You may be quite unconcerned when Tiger and Paws delicately step through the cutlery, but some guests will literally gag at the thought of sitting down at a table a cat or two has walked across. Cats also have an uncanny ability to find the one person in the room who hates them. Having spotted this person, they invariably leap into her lap. Unless you know all your guests share your love of felines, yours should be scarce at a party. As with Fifi, lock Tiger and Paws away, putting them into the room where their litter box is kept.

Accidents

These happen, as we all know. When a guest has one, whether it is to spill his red wine on your white linen tablecloth or to burn a hole in your Aubusson carpet with his cigarette ash, you are to act as if it doesn't matter at all. You are gracious, kind, putting him at ease and assuring him that it is nothing to be concerned about. At the same time, you certainly may whisk out the club soda and apply it before a stain sets, explaining as you do that he will see that everything is just fine as soon as the bubbles go to work, or whatever. If there is nothing you need to do but there is a big stain, you could cover it with a napkin to put him out of the embarrassment and distress looking at it might cause him. You may not cry, look aghast or snarl at anyone who accidentally spills or breaks something.

Children

While I believe that children should be exposed to the preparation and festivities involved in their parents' entertainments, I also believe they should be so exposed briefly, unless the party includes other children. They may take coats at the door, pass hors d'oeuvres and chat for a few minutes with guests, but then they should be provided their own entertainment in another room. For small children, this means hiring a babysitter to play with them and put them to bed. For older children, this means renting a video, finding a good book, or simply going to bed themselves.

Children should not be asked to play the piano, tap dance or sing for the guests, presuming that your party has not been held as a showcase for their talents. These activities should be reserved for grandparents and close friends at another time.

Should a guest arrive with her children (something no one

should *ever* do unless the invitation specifically included them) there is nothing you can do but welcome them, provide refreshment and cope. If your table cannot seat another person, you can set up trays or a table in the kitchen if they haven't eaten, and then perhaps direct them, with their mother to assist, to a family room or bedroom to watch television or play. If they wish to remain at their mother's side, it is her situation to deal with and you can do no more than your best to offer them entertainment of their own.

Unexpected Guests

When someone arrives with an unexpected guest (an appalling breach of etiquette), you can do nothing but welcome them warmly and readjust your plans. If your party is a buffet dinner or cocktail party where there are no set places, one more person shouldn't make a difference. When it is a seated dinner for twelve and he makes thirteen, you have to do the best you can to make room for one more.

Should an invited guest call and ask, at the last minute, if he can bring a friend, you certainly can deny the request if you simply don't have room, but if you do, you would kindly extend your invitation to include the new visitor.

I sincerely hope that your own entertaining dilemmas are few and far between, for the pleasure of entertaining graciously and well is a great one. It is one which enables you to use all your creative talents in the planning of an environment and ambience that welcomes guests to your home to share very special times with one another and with you. While the etiquette of table manners, whether the table is a formal dinner table or a picnic bench outdoors, provides the structure for your entertaining moments, it is the food you serve, the conversation that ensues, the happiness that is generated and the wonderful time that is had by all that provides the lasting memories for you and your guests. These pleasures are made possible by the most important etiquette guideline of all, which asks only that each of us treat others as we would wish to be treated ourselves. This caring philosophy keeps the broken glass, the inappropriate attire, the overcooked beans or the mismatched forks from seeming any more significant than they really are. It keeps the focus on guests, who immediately feel at home and comfortable, knowing that they are fortunate, indeed, to be sharing your hospitality.

3

Table-Setting
Environments:

From Formal to Family Style

If the ketchup bottle has become your standard centerpiece, it's time to reconsider what you want your table to be. If you do most of the cooking in your home, in only a few years you've prepared and served thousands of breakfasts, lunches and dinners. Many cooks say they have a hard enough time planning varied menus—presentation is their last priority. I understand this sentiment, for I've been a homemaker for many more than just a few years. I empathize with the temptation to move the ketchup bottle, or the mustard jar, directly from the refrigerator to the table. It's a temptation I've always resisted, however, for I believe that any mealtime, no matter how informal, must be an oasis in the frenzy which surrounds us.

As discussed in Chapter One, even the most casual of family dinners should provide pleasure to more than the sense of taste. Although a condiment dish is just one more piece to get out, fill, empty, wash and put away again, it adds to the pleasing appearance your table should have. Not pleasing is a mustard jar with a knife stuck in it. Not pleasing is a jar of pickles, fork handle protruding. Salt shakers and pepper grinders should not feel sticky; table linens should not be stained, etc. The "nots" are self-evident. What we all can forget is that these "nots" are also important and detract from even the most perfectly cooked meal.

Several years ago we were invited to the home of some new acquaintances for dinner. The meal itself was delicious. It was a large dinner party, and the maid who served was efficient and skilled. Care had been put into a creative mixing of china and silver. But on the table were four bottles of salad dressing, straight from the shelf at the grocery store. This did not ruin the dinner party but it did ruin the appearance of the otherwise perfectly set table. How much more attractive it would have been had the hostess presented the dressings in small serving dishes arranged on a tray to be passed together and spooned, not poured, onto salads. Generally, salads are dressed and tossed in the kitchen, particularly for a formal dinner, but if you choose to offer a choice of dressings, do take the time to present them attractively.

At another dinner, the hostess had arranged a beautiful floral centerpiece. It was so full, however, that guests had to crane their necks to see one another, and attempts at conversation were actually absurd, with diners peering between roses just to attempt eye contact. And at another otherwise lovely dinner party, while the centerpiece was in proportion to the table, giant candelabra loomed over everything, practically touching the chandelier. In other words, proportion is another major table-setting consideration.

Also important are cleanliness—from napery to flatware—color, fragrance (the dinner table is *not* the place for heavily scented candles), light and sound. When all the senses are pleased, your table becomes the perfect "stage" for all the thought and care you have expended in the kitchen. It becomes, as well, the environment that provides relaxation and a forum for all who are present to enjoy one another's company, to practice consideration for one another, and to ultimately leave feeling refreshed and better for having been there.

THE ENVIRONMENT

Making those at your table comfortable is the first prerequisite for creating a desirable environment. Air, light, noise or sound and space are some of the components to consider.

When the weather is stifling, and air-conditioning is not available, fans should be considered, even on a patio or deck, to create a gentle breeze and to keep air circulating. It is difficult to feel much like eating in ovenlike conditions.

For breakfast, brunch, lunch and tea, bright and light matches the cheerful atmosphere at which these mealtimes occur. For suppers and dinners, low lighting, but not so low as to make your meal difficult to see, provided by dimmed lamps, candles or both, creates a calm, relaxed atmosphere.

Sound should never be jarring. Save noisy vocal recordings, improvisational jazz and rock music for other occasions. If you enjoy background music with a meal, it should be pleasant but unobtrusive. Chopin, Mozart, classical guitar and piano or Bach pieces are all examples of dinner music that accompanies a meal but doesn't overwhelm it. Of course if you are hosting a luau, Hawaiian island music is just the thing to play, and Italian country ballads or even opera themes lend festivity to your pasta party.

The last component, space, is a sometimes overlooked consideration. Never squeeze more people than can fit comfortably at your table. Comfortable means not sitting with arms hugged to the body. It means room to cut without banging elbows, room to pull one's chair close enough to the table and room to allow service if there is serving help. Twenty-four inches is usually adequate distance between each place setting, thirty inches if there is table service and chairs are high-backed, to allow servers to present dishes at the side of each diner. If chairs have narrow and low backs, people can sit much closer together. This is especially true of a small, round table, the curve of which leaves a spreading wedge of space between the chairs at the back even if the seats touch at the front corners.

If you are inviting more people than your table can fit easily, consider using two or three smaller tables. Don't limit yourself to the dining room—look at a large hallway, a corner of the living room, a family room, or a porch or deck as possibilities for additional tables. Without party help, scattered tables work best for a buffet dinner. After guests have helped themselves, they find seating wherever you have placed tables.

TABLE LINENS

Tablecloths

Except for the most formal tables when actual linen, damask or lace tablecloths are used, table coverings can be as varied as there are colors, patterns and textures.

If the tablecloth is of white damask, which is best for a truly formal dinner, a pad must be put under it. If you do not have a felt pad cut to the dimensions of your table, a folded white blanket serves very well. Damask is the most conservative tablecloth, suitable in any dining room from English or French style to contemporary. Embroidered or lace-inserted tablecloths are appropriate for low-ceilinged, old-fashioned rooms. Either lace or linen goes over the table without felt or other padding.

When a damask or linen cloth is used, the middle crease must be put on so that it is an absolutely straight and unwavering line down the exact center from head to foot of the table. If it is an embroidered cloth be sure the embroidery or monogram is right side up.

The tablecloth for a seated dinner should hang down from fifteen to eighteen inches at the most. It should *not* extend to the floor as it does on a buffet table.

No matter how concerned you are about soiling your beautiful—possibly heirloom—damask cloth, *never* cover it with clear plastic. Not only does it have an unpleasant, slippery surface, but the beauty of the cloth cannot possibly be clearly seen, and you might just as well buy an imitation plastic cloth or use a painting tarp and leave the other in the drawer! With today's cleaning processes, there are few spots that cannot be removed, and those who are fortunate enough to have lovely table linens should not hide them away, but should use them, for their own enjoyment and to the delight of their guests.

Linens for less formal meals should complement the rest of your table service—if your china is a busy print, your tablecloth should not be another busy print, but a stripe or pin dot might work beautifully when there is a common color theme. If your tableware is plain, any number of prints and colors could be used. The only limit is your own creativity and available materials. Sheets and quilts are examples of alternatives to regular tablecloths.

Place Mats

When your table is a thing of beauty in and of itself, place mats instead of a tablecloth allow you to show off the table surface and to create individual places for guests.

As with tablecloths, alternatives needn't be real place mats— rectangles of fabric, round paper doilies slightly larger than the plate and small linen dish towels—are all examples of creative alternatives to purchased place mats.

Napkins

A truly formal damask dinner napkin matches the tablecloth and is approximately twenty-four inches square. Whether your napkins are that size or not, they are folded in this manner:

Very large napkins are folded three times in each direction to make a smaller square. The two sides are then folded under, making a loosely "rolled rectangle." The napkin is not flattened

Napkin folded to form a loosely rolled rectangle allowing monogram to appear in lower left hand corner. Napkin folded diagonally allowing monogram to show in the center point.

down completely. Care must be taken so that any monogram shows at the lower left corner of the rectangle, or if the initials are at the center of one side of the napkins, that they appear in the center third of the "roll."

Smaller napkins may be folded in the same way, making only two folds to form the smaller square. Or the littler square may be folded in half *diagonally*, and the two points folded under, leaving the monogram showing in the center point. *(See page 106 for ways to fold luncheon napkins.)*

Napkins are placed in the center of the service plate with the monogram facing the diner. They are put at the side only when a first course is put on the table before seating the guests or if the dinner is informal and there is no service plate. To put the napkins at the side of the empty plate simply in order to display the plate is incorrect for formal table-setting.

Napkins are never placed *under* the forks. Since the napkin is the first thing the diner uses when seated, it makes no sense to bury it under cutlery.

The old custom of wrapping a dinner roll in the napkin was most impractical and, fortunately, is passé. When the diner flicked open the napkin he generally also flicked the roll right onto the floor.

A napkin may be folded in pleats and placed in an empty goblet so that the edges fan out.

The placement of napkins can add a decorative touch to your table. A napkin, fanned from an empty goblet, can be very pretty, but should be done only if there is a servant to then fill the goblet. If this presentation is done and the host or hostess must then circle the table filling goblets as guests remove their napkins, it is hardly worth the effect.

For other than the most formal dinners, napkin rings may be used. If you have napkin rings, the napkin may be pulled through and placed at the left of the forks or in the center of the service plate. If your napkin rings are not complementary to your table decor, try tying a ribbon in a bow around the napkin.

Napkins are *never* put back in the ring at the end of the meal unless it is a family meal or you have houseguests and napkins are reused two or three times. Rather they are smoothed into loose folds and placed on the table at the end of the meal, after

A napkin may be drawn through a napkin ring and placed at the left of the fork or in the center of the service plate.

the hostess places her napkin on the table. Used napkins are not put on top of the plate.

SILVER

The silver used at a formal dinner should be sterling, or at least should appear to be sterling. Often silver plated flatware is substituted and generally is available in all the same pieces and sizes as is sterling.

It is not necessary that *all* silver match, although all forks, spoons and knives at one place setting should be of the same pattern. Dessert silver, which is usually not on the table but is brought in with the dessert plates at a formal dinner, need not match the dinner forks, and after-dinner coffee spoons are frequently entirely different. Knives and forks should match, unless you happen to have a set of knives with crystal or carved-bone handles that may be used with any pattern. Serving pieces need not match flatware, although they should be silver if the meal is formal, never wooden, bamboo or plastic.

Silver serving dishes complement the most formal table and its table linens, crystal and china. Frequently referred to as hollow ware, they are made in two grades of metals and are silver-plated. One grade is made from refined nickel silver and is plated with pure silver. The other is a composition of tin, antimony and copper. It is less durable than nickel silver.

Flatware and Serving Pieces

There are a few variations on a theme when selecting appropriate flatware. Differences are shown here:

Dinner Fork. The largest fork at a place setting, used especially when meat is served.

Dinner or Large Knife. Accompanies dinner fork.

Steak Knife. A sharp serated-edged knife brought to the table for the meat course if needed.

Smaller Fork and Knife. These utensils are often referred to as luncheon, salad or dessert fork and knife. They are used for any course except the meat course when used at dinner but are also used at breakfast and lunch. Fork may be used for dessert, alone or with a dessert spoon. Can also be used for salad. When there are no fish knives and forks, this set is used for a fish course, as well.

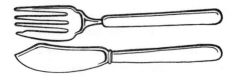

Fish Knife and Fork. A fixture in older silver services. Is replaced by smaller fork and knife when not available.

Fruit Knife. Used when a fruit or fruit and cheese course is served to peel and cut fruit.

Butter Knife or Butter Spreader. Set at each place on the bread-and-butter plate. If not enough individual spreaders, butter is placed on serving plate to be passed at the table.

Oyster or Seafood Fork. A small three-pronged fork designed for eating shrimp cocktail, oysters and clams, it is sometimes called a cocktail fork.

Soup Spoon. A small round spoon used for soup served in cups. Or a large oblong spoon used for desserts, ice cream and often for cereal. This versatile spoon also may be used as small serving piece.

Teaspoon. Used with tea, standard-size coffee cups and mugs and soup served in cups, for cut fruit and for dessert served in dessert glasses.

Coffee Spoon. This small spoon is used for demitasse or small coffee cups.

Dessert Spoon. Same as large soup spoon. May also be used for soup instead of soup spoon.

Serving Spoon. Used mainly as a serving spoon for vegetables, cut fruit, berries, trifles, other desserts.

Iced-Tea Spoon. Long-handled teaspoon used for iced beverages served in tall glasses.

Flatware Placement

The rules for the placement of flatware are based on use. The first pieces to be used are on the outside. Forks are placed at the left of the plate, with the exception of the oyster fork which is placed to the right of the soup spoon. All knives and spoons are set to the right of the plate except the butter spreader or butter knife which is placed on the bread-and-butter plate diagonally from top left to bottom right. Knives are placed with the cutting edge facing the plate.

No matter how extensive the menu, no more than three forks should be set at the left and three knives and the oyster fork at the right for a total of four forks, including the oyster fork, and four knives, including a butter spreader. If more pieces are required, they should be brought to the table with the course with which they are to be used.

When soup and a fruit cup are served, the spoons for these courses are placed to the right of the knives with the one to be used first placed to the outside. The seafood or oyster fork is placed to the right of the spoon, in this case.

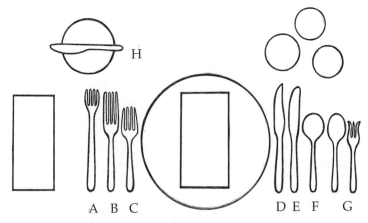

At a formal dinner, a place setting of silver would look like this, beginning at the left of the plate: A, First course fork. B, Main course fork. C, Salad fork. Moving to the right out from the plate D, Main course knife. E, First course knife. F, Soup spoon. G, Fruit cup spoon or seafood fork. H, Butter spreader.

If salad is served American-style as a first course, the salad fork would be the one farthest from the plate on the left; when served as a second course, it would be placed between the first-course fork and the main-course fork.

Dessert flatware, when not brought with the dessert may be treated one of two ways. American-style is placed at the top of the place setting parallel to the table edge with the fork handle to the left and the spoon handle to the right, while European-style is to have the bowls of the dessert fork and spoon both facing left. (See Chapter Four, page 159, "Don't Drink from the Fingerbowl!" for the presentation of dessert flatware when finger bowls are used.)

Spoons for coffee served after dessert come with the service at that time if coffee is served at the table. They are placed on the saucer and passed with the cup if coffee is served elsewhere.

Serving Pieces

Many flatware pieces can do double duty as serving pieces, such as actual serving spoons, large forks, and dessert spoons. Other serving pieces have been specifically designed with certain foods in mind. Some of the more common ones are shown here:

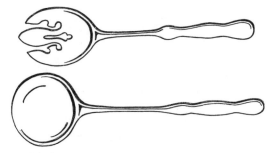

Salad Spoon and Fork. Used together to portion salad onto salad plates.

Cold Meat Fork. Used for cold-cut platters; also as large serving fork with serving spoon for lifting portions from serving dish or platter.

Serving Tongs. May be used to lift sliced meats from the serving platter onto the plate when no serving fork and spoon are provided. Also used for serving pasta and other foods more easily grasped than spooned. Silver tongs may also be used to serve salad.

Sugar Tongs. Used to lift a cube of sugar onto the saucer of a cup of coffee or tea. Sugar is then transferred with the teaspoon so that tongs never touch liquid.

Sugar Spoon. Fluted spoon used to transfer sugar from bowl to cup. Never to be used to stir; should never touch liquid.

Flat or Lasagna Server. Used to transfer portions from serving dish to plate.

Pierced Vegetable Spoon. Spoon with slots or open design work to permit any liquid to remain in the serving bowl when vegetables are transferred to the plate.

Jellied Cranberry Server. Thin edge is used to slice a portion of cranberry; flat side used to transfer from serving dish to plate.

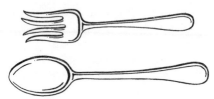

Serving Spoon and Fork. Larger than regular serving spoon and dinner fork; used together to transfer meats and vegetables difficult to transfer with a spoon alone. Portion is lifted with the spoon on the bottom and balanced by the fork on top.

Salt Spoons. Tiny spoons used with open saltcellars.

Ladles. Larger ladles are used for soup and punch; smaller ones for gravies and sauces.

Pastry Server. Used to lift a piece of cut pie or cake to the dessert plate.

Hollow ware

The most often used hollow ware at formal parties are coffee and tea services, which include a large tray, a coffee pot, a teapot, a sugar bowl and a cream pitcher. Silver sugar tongs or a silver sugar spoon must be used with a silver coffee or tea service.

Other silver serving dishes are compotes for fruits, nuts and candies; a pitcher for water or other beverages; a bread tray, generally lined with a napkin; a covered butter dish; a gravy boat; a wine cooler; a silver bowl used for salad, fruit, and sometimes with flowers as a centerpiece; vegetable dishes; and platters. Hollow ware is also used for candlesticks and candelabra on formal tables; for salt and pepper shakers and salt cellars; for trays; and on buffet tables, for chafing dish holders.

STAINLESS STEEL FLATWARE AND SERVING PIECES

For everyday use and for more casual entertaining, stainless steel flatware and serving pieces appropriately accompany earthenware chinaware and regular glassware. Because its use is less formal, stainless steel tableware is manufactured only in basic sizes for general use and most frequently includes a dinner knife and fork, a teaspoon, and a small fork for salad or dessert. Also included are serving spoons, the smaller size of which may be used as soup spoons. Such extras as pickle forks and jellied cranberry servers are seldom found with stainless steel sets—unlike sterling silver flatware which is sold by the place setting, stainless steel flatware is generally sold by sets of 6, 8, 10 or 12 place settings.

CHINA

It is interesting to note that the word "china" was first used in England to describe porcelain pieces simply because the first pieces to be seen came from China. As it is used today, the word should describe only porcelain dinnerware. Porcelain china is divided into three groups; soft-paste, hard-paste and bone china, which is classified between the other two and is made with calcined bone dust. The classifications refer to the process by which the pieces are made.

Pottery pieces should be referred to as earthenware or stone china, because although glazed, they are not made with a porcelain process. They are fired at a lower temperature than china, and the ingredients, although similar, are combined with different proportions. Pottery pieces are porous, while china pieces are not.

Ceramic is a term used for anything made from baked clay but is not used to refer to table china.

China Patterns

China patterns may be mixed at the table, but *all* the plates for each course at one table should match. For example, all the service plates must be of one pattern, although the dinner plates, while matching each other, may be entirely different. Silver or glass butter plates and glass salad or dessert plates may be used with any fine china. The most important consideration is that each item be of the same quality as the others. It is entirely incorrect, for example, to use heavy pottery salad plates with fine china dinner plates, just as it is to use paper napkins with a damask tablecloth.

Service Plates

At the most formal dinner parties, a service plate is put at every place when the table is set. Service plates are usually twelve inches in diameter and are the "base" for the first course, which is served on separate plates that are put on top of the service plates.

When the first course is finished, these plates are removed

and the second course served, again on separate plates, which are again placed on top of the service plates. When the entrée is the next course, the previous course served is removed with the service plate and warm dinner plates are passed.

Service plates are not used at an informal dinner, except under the stemmed glass used for shrimp cocktail, fruit cocktail, etc., and under soup plates. In this case, the service plate may be simply another dinner or dessert plate—whichever size and style is most appropriate. It is removed with the course, and warmed dinner plates are placed at each table setting or in front of the host or hostess if one of them is serving.

Additional Dishes

Even at a completely informal meal, separate plates should be provided for salad and for bread and butter. It does your dinner no justice if a crisp cool salad must be put on a hot plate or one swimming in gravy.

BREAD AND BUTTER PLATES

The bread-and-butter plate is placed to the upper left of the dinner plate so that it is close to the tines of the outside fork. Breads are passed in a flat dish or a basket. A guest helps himself with his fingers and lays the roll or bread on his bread-and-butter plate. Whenever a guest has no bread left at his place, more should be passed to him. Except at formal dinners, bread and other condiments are usually passed around the table by the guests themselves.

Butter may be cut up into individual pats and placed in a small bowl which is placed on an underplate. If your silverware includes one, a seafood fork should be provided, since it is easier to spear the pats than to try to lift them with a knife. The fork is left on or returned to the underdish when the butter is passed, not left on top of the butter.

SALAD PLATES

The salad plate is placed to the left of the dinner plate, almost touching the bread-and-butter plate. Only when salad is served as a separate course should the salad plate be placed directly on the service plate.

When salad is served at a party where there is no help, it is best that the guests pass the bowl, each one in turn holding it for the person at his right.

SERVING DISHES

Serving dishes need not match the china or earthenware pattern of the plates, but they must be of the same genre—silver serving bowls do not belong with pottery plates, nor do wooden salad bowls belong with fine china dinnerware.

When serving dishes are to be passed, be sure they have not just come from the oven or someone is sure to suffer burned fingers in the attempt to transfer a hot dish to the next person. If they are hot offer guests a folded napkin to pass these dishes.

CONDIMENT DISHES

If there is a choice of two or three sauces or other condiments, placing them together in a divided dish, or on a small, easily managed tray, ensures that they are passed together and that all guests are aware of the choices. As with other service, dishes are passed counterclockwise from left to right.

WASTE DISHES

Meals at which foods that create their own refuse are served require the placement of waste dishes on the table. Such foods include lobsters, clams, other shellfish, ribs and corn on the cob.

Waste dishes keep dinner plates from becoming piled with

residue. At a *very* informal dinner, large bowls can be placed between guests. When space permits, each guest should be given a waste dish of his or her own. This would be placed above the bread-and-butter plate to the left of the dinner plate.

SALT AND PEPPER

Although some hosts would prefer not to have salt and pepper on the table, believing the food is seasoned as they wish it to be eaten, it is a good idea to have them nearby since someone will invariably ask for them.

Salt and pepper may be served in matching mills, in sterling or crystal shakers, or in other containers designed for dispensing them. They may also be served in pepper pots and saltcellars. (See "Salt in a Saltcellar," page 144 for the proper way to use saltcellars.)

Pepper pots and saltcellars should be at every place or between every two places. For a dinner of twelve there should be six (and never less than four) salts and peppers.

ASHTRAYS

Most hostesses prefer that their guests do not smoke at least until coffee is served, and no ashtrays or cigarettes are placed on the table. When this is so, the guests should have the good sense and courtesy to refrain until after dinner.

CRYSTAL

When glassware is placed on the table, a sparkle is added, as is another dimension in height. Crystal adds to sensory pleasure at the table. Visually it catches the light. To the touch and taste, it adds enjoyment. Think how much less the experience would be if champagne were served in earthenware mugs—there is something about seeing its bubbles and shimmer through crystal that makes it all the more special.

There is stemware for different kinds of wine, with shape and style adding to or detracting from the contents. Tinted wine glasses are very pretty, but the true connoisseur prefers to see the color of the wine. The table-decorating artist loves the addition of color to the table through tinted glassware. Neither is incorrect, although clear crystal is most appropriate for very formal dinners.

Cut glass can be beautiful, but does not do for a brandy snifter where the heat of the hand is supposed to warm the brandy through thin crystal, and should be reserved for water goblets.

There are reasons for the differing lengths of the "stems" of glassware. The shorter stem of a brandy glass enables the hand

German   Alsace   Bordeaux

Glassware designed for particular wines is identified by its shape. From the left: White-wine glasses include German and Alsace. Red-wine glasses are identified by

to cup the bowl. The longer stem of the wine glass *prevents* the hand from warming the wine and changing its temperature.

As with silver and china, all glasses placed on the table do not have to be from a matched set. They should match in weight and kind, however. A pottery wine glass does not belong with a cut-glass water goblet. It never belongs on a formal table.

The variety in crystal is boundless—many European wine regions have overseen the design of glasses specifically for their wines. Some of them are illustrated below and if your budget and storage space permits, it is lovely to have each type for each kind of wine you serve. In truth, however, it is only necessary to have four basic shapes and sizes, even for the most formal din-

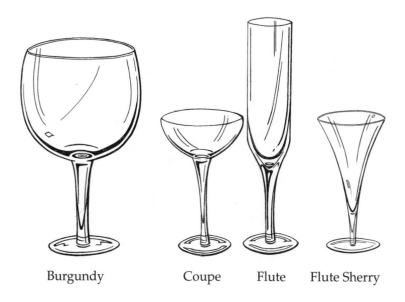

Burgundy   Coupe   Flute   Flute Sherry

shape for Bordeaux and for Burgundy. Also shown are a champagne coupe, a champagne flute and a flute sherry.

ner. These are a white wine glass, a red wine glass, a champagne flute or flat glass and a sherry glass. A water goblet is a fifth glass that accompanies the other crystal.

Each place at the table should be set with the number of glasses that will be used during the meal, with the exception of the dessert wine glass, which is put on the table when the dessert is served. A champagne glass or flute should be on the table from the beginning of the meal, even if champagne is not served until the end of the meal.

Water goblets are placed closest to the center of each setting, just above and to the right of the knife, with the wine glasses set to the right of the water goblet with height being more important than order. If space does not permit a straight line of glassware, it may be arranged in a triangle shape, with the smallest glass to the front.

Water glasses are filled only two-thirds and wine glasses only halfway, never to the top.

There should be separate wine glasses for each different wine you are serving. *Never* pour another kind of wine into a glass that has already been used for a different one.

Wine glasses are filled only about halfway, and water goblets about two-thirds. Never fill any glass to the top.

All crystal should be spotless. Be sure to allow enough time to wipe glasses with a lint-free cloth and remove all smudges and spots.

(See "Place Settings" on page 93 for the arrangement of glassware on the table.)

THE CENTERPIECE

The first piece to be put on the table once the cloth is in place is the centerpiece. As its name implies, it must be in the exact center. It must never be so high that the diners cannot see over it, but its length and width are limited only by the size of your table. It can be composed of a wide variety of things—fresh flowers being the most common and surely one of the loveliest. Plastic flowers are out of place, but lovely glass, china or silk imitation flowers or fruit are appropriate. Carefully arranged fruit makes a beautiful centerpiece, as does something as simple as a savoy cabbage, when the table setting is not perfectly formal. Ornaments that need neither fruit nor flowers can be effective, too. Two of my own particular favorites are a covered china tureen decorated with charming shells and fish, and a pair of large crystal fish, which I use with glass candlesticks.

When table space permits, setting small vases containing one tulip, or a small bouquet, before each guest adds charm. Even a simple, outdoor luncheon table should have a centerpiece—a pottery vase filled with zinnias, and two bright, small vases placed at diagonally opposite sides of it, between place settings—a pyramid of strawberries—a basket of lemons and oranges—anything that adds visual attraction and complements the rest of the table setting.

Sometimes the centerpiece can become token gifts for your guests. Such things as an arrangement of tiny potted cactuses in a basket or tiny pots of pansies can be given to parting guests as a token of your thanks for their presence.

CANDLES AND CANDELABRA

Candles for the most formal dinner should be white and brand new. Only if you are skilled with a candle-tip shaper and there is no evidence of smoke or drips, might a used candle be permissible.

Candles are lighted before the guests come to the table and remain lighted until they leave the dining room. They are not to be lighted before twilight at the earliest, or slightly before if the day is gloomy and light is dim. They may be placed on a luncheon table, but only as an ornament.

When the centerpiece is in place, a pair of candlesticks is placed at each end, about halfway between the centerpiece and the end of the table, or candelabra at either end halfway between the places of the host and hostess and the centerpiece. The number of candles depends upon whether the dining room is otherwise lighted or not. If the candles alone light the table, there should be a candle for each person. You will need two or four candelabra, depending on the length of the table and the number of guests. If there are two candelabra at each end, they are spaced evenly between the centerpiece and the host's and hostess's places. But if the candles are merely ornaments, two or four candles will be adequate for a table of up to eight. Candlesticks or candelabra must be high and the candles as long as the proportion can stand so that the light does not shine into the eyes of those at the table.

Whether perfectly formal or very casual, a dinner table can

be enhanced by candles as the centerpiece itself. A row of crystal candlesticks in varying heights—groupings of candles in the center of the table—candles in pottery holders—the arrangements and possibilities add creativity and appeal to the table.

Candles should be extinguished with a candle snuffer. If they must be blown out, be sure to hold your cupped hand behind the flame so hot wax doesn't splatter on your table or linens.

PLACE CARDS

Place cards are about three-quarters of an inch high when folded, by two and one-half inches long, usually plain or bordered in silver or gold. Decorated cards, while suitable on such special occasions as Christmas or a birthday, are out of place on a formal table. Some hostesses have their cards monogrammed in silver or gold, and a family that uses a crest may have the crest engraved at the top.

The courtesy title and surname—"Miss Moore," "Mr. Thompson"—are used at official dinners except when there is more than one guest with the same surname, in which case, "Mr. Benjamin Franklin" and "Mr. George Franklin," for example, should be used to make the distinction. At a party of friends or relatives first names are used, or if necessary to differentiate, "Helen M." and "Helen G." The writing should be large enough to be seen easily by the guests.

Place cards may be put on top of and in the center of the napkin, but if unsteady there, they may be placed on the tablecloth above the service plate at the exact center of the place setting.

When it is appropriate to use decorative place cards, your imagination can again assist in creating delightful additions to your table. These need not be expensive, and it is often fun for children to participate in the preparation, practicing both their artistry and their penmanship. One charming example I observed was created for Easter. Small bunnies were made from magnolia pods that had dropped to the ground. The children cut them to create a round head which was glued to the left side of each place card, and shaped ears which were glued to the top of the fold and extended above the place card. Each person's name was then written in a pastel marker the colors of the table linens. To complete the theme a basket of dyed eggs was used as a centerpiece.

MENU CARDS

Most often seen at official dinners or banquets, menu cards are once in a while seen at a formal dinner in a private home. Usually there is only one, which is placed in front of the host, but sometimes there is one between every two guests.

The menu card never includes obvious accessories such as celery, olives, rolls, jelly, chocolates or fruit, any more than it would include salt and pepper or iced water.

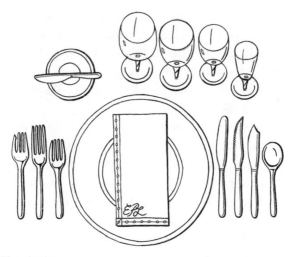

Formal Place Setting.

PLACE SETTINGS

Formal Dinners

The service plates, with the pattern properly positioned so that the "picture" faces the diner, are first put around the table at equal distances. The silver is placed in the order of its use, with the implements to be used first farthest from the plate. The salad fork (as shown in the illustration on page 92) is placed next to the left of the plate, then the meat fork to its left, and outermost the fish fork, which will be used first. Just to the right of the plate is the salad knife, to its right is the meat knife, and on the outside is the fish knife. All knives are placed with the cutting edge of each toward the plate. Outside the knives are the soup spoon and/or fruit spoon, and beyond the spoons, the oyster fork if shellfish is to be served. Recall that the oyster (or shellfish) fork, is the only fork ever to be placed on the right.

No more than three of any implement are *ever* placed on the table (with the exception of the oyster fork's making four forks

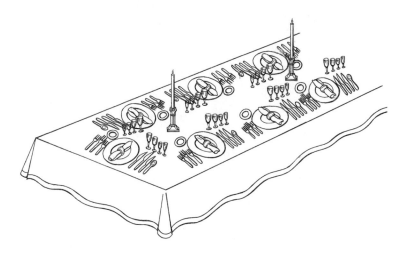

Formal Dinner Table.

and the butter spreader making four knives). Therefore, if more than three courses are served before dessert, the fork for the fourth course is brought in at the time the course is served. Or the salad knife and fork may be omitted in the beginning and may be brought in when salad is served.

The placement for bread-and-butter plates and salad plates is described above, as is the placement for water goblets and wine glasses.

At a formal dinner everything on the table should be symmetrically and evenly spaced.

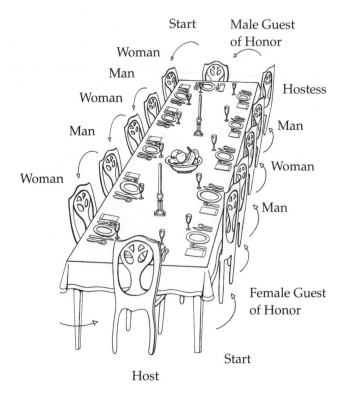

Seating arrangement for a party of eight, twelve or sixteen. To avoid seating two men and two women together the hostess moves one place to the left so that the male guest of honor sits opposite the host. Arrows indicate order of service.

SEATING ARRANGEMENTS AT THE FORMAL TABLE

Part of any host's or hostess's table planning must include seating. This is one of the first things that should be done to ensure that the table is large enough to accommodate the number of guests you intend to invite.

When you are seating three, five or seven couples, there is no problem at all. It works out evenly, with the hostess at one end of the table (usually the end nearest the kitchen), the host opposite her, and the men and women alternating on either side. However, when you have multiples of four you must

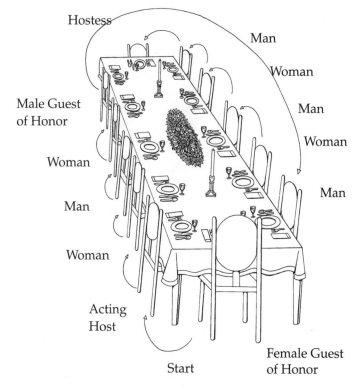

The correct seating arrangement for a group that has a hostess but no host. Arrows indicate order of service.

make another arrangement. To avoid seating two women and two men together, the hostess moves one place to the left, so that the man on her right sits opposite the host at the end of the table.

When a single person entertains, she must do her best to alternate her male and female guests in so far as possible. Illustrated here is the seating for a single hostess. The male guest of honor sits to her right and the female guest of honor sits opposite her. Service then begins with the female guest of honor and continues to her left until the male guest of honor is served. The servant then serves the man to the female guest of honor's right and continues down the opposite side of the table, serving the hostess last.

Informal Dinners

The main difference between the formal and informal place setting is that for the latter there is less of everything. There are fewer courses served, so fewer pieces of silver are set out.

Informal three-course dinner place setting, as the diner arrives to be seated.

Generally only one—at the most, two—wines are served, so a water goblet and one (or two) wine glasses are all that are necessary. Frequently wine is not served at all, and iced-tea glasses or simply tumblers for water or mugs for beer are used. If bread or rolls are to be served, a bread-and-butter plate should be used. If you do not have butter plates to match your dinner plates try to buy a set of glass ones. It is less than appetizing to have one's bread or roll get soggy and messy because it has slid into the juice or salad dressing on your dinner plate, or to see the pat of butter on the edge of the warm plate melting rapidly down into your meat or vegetables before you can spread it on your bread.

For more or less the same reason, serve separate salad plates if your menu includes any dishes with gravy. Salad may be put on the same plate with broiled steak or chops or chicken, perhaps, but an unappetizing mess results when it is combined with lamb stew!

The typical place setting for an informal three-course dinner would include:

2 forks—one for dinner at the far left, and one for dessert or salad to the left of the plate

dinner plate—not on the table when guests sit down if being warmed in the kitchen

salad plate—to the left of the forks

1 knife—next to the plate on the right—if for steak, chops, chicken, or game birds, it may be a steak knife

2 spoons—dessert spoon to the right of the knife, and a soup spoon at the far right

1 butter plate with butter knife—if you have them; 1 butter plate alone if you haven't butter knives

1 water goblet—or tall tumbler

1 wine glass—if you plan to serve wine

napkin—in the center of the plate or to the left of the forks

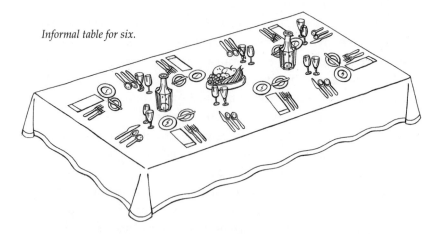

Informal table for six.

Only if you plan to serve coffee with the meal should coffee cups and saucers be placed on the table before dinner begins. If so, they go to the right of the setting with the coffee spoon on the right side of the saucer.

Service plates are not used at an informal dinner, except under the stemmed glass used for shrimp cocktail, fruit cocktail, etc., and under soup plates. It need not be a true service plate but may be another dinner or dessert plate.

The dinner plate should not be on the table when your guests sit down, because it should be very warm when the food is served. If you have help, the maid passes the hot plates around before she starts serving. If you are having a seated buffet the stack of warm plates is on the buffet table.

The dessert spoon and fork (or if you prefer, just a spoon) need not be beside the plate. They can be brought in, as at a formal dinner, with the dessert plate, or they can be placed, American style, above the center of the place setting, horizontally with the bowl of the spoon facing left and the tines of the fork facing right (as shown on page 152).

You may use any materials that appeal to you on your informal table. Wooden salt and pepper grinders, pewter plates, wooden salad bowls, ironware, pottery and stainless steel "silver" all are fine. However, each item must be in keeping with the others. Don't combine plastic wine glasses with fine bone china, or plastic plates with delicate crystal glasses. You may, however, use wooden salad bowls with pottery or "everyday" chinaware plates, or glass salad plates with stoneware dinner plates. The secret is not in having everything of one design, but in creating, out of a variety of patterns and colors, a harmonious whole.

When your guests arrive at the table, the butter should already be on the butter plates, the water glasses filled, and the wine, if served, in a cooler beside the host, on a coaster on the table, or in a decanter on the table. Salad is often served with the main course instead of as a separate course, and for reasons already discussed, a separate salad plate or bowl is a must.

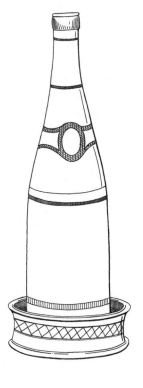

The wine bottle may be placed on the table, on a coaster near the host. If the table is large, a second bottle should be placed at the other end of the table.

Ashtrays, if used, salts and peppers, and condiments in serving dishes must all be in place, conveniently spaced around the table.

BUFFET TABLES

The basic principle of buffet table setting is that only necessary and useful objects are used. Unless there is ample space, omit articles that are solely ornamental. Flowers in the center of the table are lovely, of course, but if it is a question of choosing between decorative flowers and edible fruit, a centerpiece of the fruit to be served for dessert is preferable.

In the same way, if the table is crowded and candles are not needed to see by, they are better left off. If candles are needed, candelabra are better than candlesticks because first, they give

Buffet table in the center of the room. Arrows indicate traffic pattern around the table.

better light, and second, they are less likely to be knocked over by a guest reaching for a plate of food.

If the party is large it is better to leave the table in the center of the room so that two lines of guests may serve themselves at once. Then the most important dish is divided into two parts, and one platter or casserole placed at each end of the table. The plates are in two stacks beside them, and the napkins and silver neatly arranged next to the plates. Dishes of vegetables, salads, bread and butter, and sauces and condiments are on each side of the table so that guests need to pass down only one side—greatly speeding the service and keeping them from turning back and bumping into each other.

If the table is set against the wall, place your plates and main dish at the end that makes for the best flow of traffic. This is usually the one nearest the entrance, so that the guests, after serving themselves, do not have to double back against the people coming in.

Your buffet table may be set as formally or informally as you wish. If you use a white damask cloth, silver candelabra, and an

Buffet table against the wall. Arrows indicate traffic pattern.

elaborate centerpiece, your buffet will appear quite formal. But you can just as well go to the other extreme and use pottery dishes on a checkered tablecloth with a bowl of fruit in the center of the table. What makes your table attractive is not the elegance of the utensils and decorations you use, but the combination of dishes, linen and silver, and the way in which they are arranged.

Color plays an enormous part in the beauty of a buffet table. If you have a copper bowl or kettle to use as a centerpiece, fill it with red and yellow fruit or a combination of fall vegetables— squash, tomatoes, pumpkins for a Halloween or Thanksgiving table. Keep the autumn tints in mind: Use green, red or russet mats and yellow pottery on a bare table. Or a green or yellow tablecloth is warm and inviting. Bright red napkins and/or china set the tone for an appealing Valentine's Day table, and of course pastel pinks, yellows or blues are synonymous with springtime.

Whichever type of buffet you are serving, the most valuable piece of equipment you can have is one that keeps things hot. I recommend an electric hot plate or tray, because they can be used to heat your plates and keep your meal warm for an almost indefinite period of time. As long as a finished casserole is covered so that it will not dry out, it may be placed on a hot plate an hour or more before dinner and be as delectable when it is served as it was the moment it was taken from the oven. The only exception, of course, is a soufflé, which must be served at once. Furthermore, with an electric appliance on the buffet table, there is no need to take the dishes to the kitchen to be kept warm for second helpings. And finally, it is unnecessary to watch and replace fuel for flame-heated chafing dishes.

Beverages

Red or white wine, a punch or other cold drink, sparkling water, or beer in its cans or bottles, together with glasses, are on the sideboard or a nearby table.

If it is a seated buffet, water glasses are on the tables and are filled before the guests sit down. Wine glasses should also be at the guests' places, but they are never filled in advance. The host (or a server) passes the wine when everyone is seated, or there may be an open bottle of wine on each table to be poured by the person nearest to it.

If coffee is on the sideboard the guests may serve themselves at any time. Or the hostess, if she prefers, takes a tray set with cups, a coffee pot, cream and sugar into the living room to serve after dinner.

When there are no individual stands or tables and guests must put their glasses beside them on the floor, it is better to set the table with iced-tea glasses or highball glasses because they are steadier than goblets. If the beverage is served with ice in the glass, it should not be put down on a table unless coasters are provided.

AFTER-DINNER COFFEE

At other than a formal dinner, coffee may be served from a tray in the living room or room other than the dining room. The hostess pours, and her helper, either a servant or a friend, passes

When coffee is served in another room after dinner, the coffee tray is set like this to hold cups, saucers, spoons, a cream pitcher, a sugar bowl and a bowl of sugar substitute packets. The sugars and cream may be transferred to another tray to be presented to each person with his or her coffee cup, or the hostess may add whatever the guest prefers and pass only the cup and saucer.

the filled cup, on a tray with sugar and cream, to each guest. The tray in front of the hostess is set to hold two pots of coffee, one decaffeinated and one regular, spoons, a sugar bowl, a cream pitcher and a bowl with sugar substitute packets. If there is no helper, the hostess may ask each guest how he prefers his coffee and add milk, sugar or artificial sweetener as he requests, after which she passes him his cup and saucer.

Coffee may also be served at the table. In this case, an identical tray would be placed in front of the hostess, who would pour from her seat. Cream and sugars would be passed on a small tray, a faster system than when the hostess stops with each cup and adds milk or sugar as her guest requests.

While coffee is being served, a tray set with bottles and decanters of liqueurs, brandy and port, along with liqueur and brandy glasses may be presented. Usually the host offers a choice and pours for each guest.

AFTER-DINNER DRINKS

After-dinner drinks may be served with coffee. If coffee is served at the table, the bottles of after-dinner drinks may be placed on the table on a tray containing a variety of glasses and each guest asked which he or she would prefer. If coffee is served in the living room the tray containing the bottles and glasses is placed on the coffee table and a choice offered to each guest.

The well-stocked after-dinner drink tray includes four different types of glasses. Brandy snifters, either large or small, are for serving cognac or armagnac. Small, stemmed glasses are for sweet liqueurs. Regular wine glasses may be used for port, and small old-fashioned glasses may be used for white or green *crème de menthe* to be served over cracked ice.

LUNCHEON TABLES

Candles are not needed on a lunch table, but are sometimes used as ornaments. They should never be lighted in the daytime. The plain white tablecloth that is correct for dinner is not used for luncheon, although colored damask is acceptable. Far more often, the lunch table is set with place mats made in any variety of linen, needlework, lace or plastic. A runner, matching the mats but two or three times as long, may be used in the center of the table.

The decorations are practically the same as for dinner; flowers or an ornament in the center, and two or four dishes of fruit or candy where they look best. If the table is very large and rather too bare without candles, four small vases with flowers matching those in the centerpiece—or any other glass or silver ornaments—may be added.

The places for a large formal luncheon are set as for dinner, with a service plate, a fork, a knife or a spoon for each course. The lunch napkin, which should go well with the tablecloth, is much smaller than the dinner napkin. Generally it is folded like

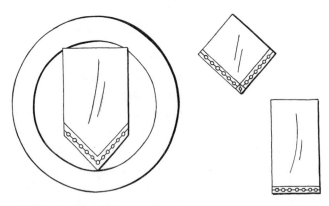

Ways to fold luncheon napkins.

a handkerchief, in a square of four thicknesses. The square is laid on the plate diagonally, with the monogrammed (or embroidered) corner pointing down toward the near edge of the table. The upper corner is then turned sharply under in a flat crease for about a quarter of its diagonal length; then the two sides are rolled loosely under, with a straight top edge and a pointed lower edge and the monogram displayed in the center. Or it can be folded in any simple way one prefers.

Luncheon place setting.

If it is a large luncheon, guests are often seated at several small tables, and place cards are used just as they are at dinner. Tables are covered with cloths, either white or colored. A small flower arrangement makes the prettiest centerpiece.

THE TEA TABLE

Those who have dining room tables use them as the simplest and most comfortable place from which to serve at a tea. However, the tea table may be set up in any room that has adequate space and easy access and egress. The guests should be able to circulate freely without becoming trapped in a corner after they have been served.

Except on a glass-topped table a cloth must always be used. It may barely cover the table, or it may hang half a yard over the edge. A tea cloth may be colored, but the conventional one is of lace or white linen with needlework, lace or appliquéd designs.

A large tea tray is set at either end of the table, one for the tea and one for the coffee.

Tea and Coffee Service.

One tray is used to bring in all the equipment necessary for the proper serving of tea: a pot with boiling water—with a flame under it if possible—a full pot of tea, tea bags if the tea is not made with loose tea, cream pitcher, sugar bowl and thin slices of lemon on a dish.

The coffee tray is simpler. The coffee is in a large urn or pot—with a flame under it. A pitcher of cream and a bowl of sugar (preferably cubes) complete the tray. If chocolate is served instead of coffee, there is nothing needed other than the pot of steaming chocolate.

The flames under the pots are not lighted before the trays are set down in order to avoid the danger of fire.

The cups and saucers are placed within easy reach of the women who are pouring, usually at the left of the tray, because they are held in the left hand while the tea (or coffee) is poured with the right. Obviously, the reverse would be true for a left-handed pourer.

On either side of the table are stacks of little tea plates, with small napkins matching the tea cloth folded on each one. Arranged behind these, or in any way that is pretty and uncluttered, are the plates of food and whatever silver is neces-sary. Forks should be on the table if cake with soft icing is served. If the table is not large enough to hold all the plates some may be placed on a sideboard or a small table in a conve-nient location.

FAMILY DINING

In times past the family dinner was an institution. It was the time when children learned table manners, the art of listening and conversing, and many other courtesies. Unfortunately few families now take advantage of this opportunity because their schedules do not permit it and in some households, because video games have been allowed to lure the youngsters away from the seated dinner; it is a great loss.

Today, I still encourage all families to enjoy special occasions periodically by setting a formal table with the prettiest table linens, china, crystal and silver. Family birthdays, the celebration of a promotion, an anniversary, an excellent report card—these are all events that warrant a full-scale celebration. This is also a way to remind your family that they are just as important as any "company" who may come to dinner—when the family never uses its prettiest things, the message is that they don't matter quite as much!

Practicality is the keynote in everyday family table settings, however. This means not only simplicity, but also, very often, kitchen dining. Often the coziest place in the house, the kitchen permits lively conversation and ease of serving. When eating at the kitchen table an extra effort should be made to make the room neat and attractive before the meal begins. If the counters are heaped with dirty pots, pans, utensils and potato peelings, the kitchen can be a pretty unappealing place to eat.

The Family Table

A minimum number of utensils is put at each place—only those absolutely necessary. Since there is usually only one course and dessert, there may be only three pieces of flatware—a fork, a knife and a spoon for the dessert. Of course, if you are having soup or fruit first, utensils for those foods must be added. You do not need to bother with separate salad forks, although individual salad bowls or plates should be set out, even at the family table. Butter plates and knives may be omitted, although if you have a dishwasher the extra plate is more than worth the trouble of putting it in the rack.

Frozen dinners and other prepared dishes should not be eaten from the containers, but should be spooned out onto warm plates.

Milk glasses should be filled before the meal, or the milk should be served in a pitcher. Other beverages should also be poured before the family is called to dinner. If, despite my introduction to this chapter, it is simply easier to serve ketchup, jelly, pickles, mustard, etc. from their jars, please at least put the jars on plates or saucers and allocate a separate serving spoon or fork for each, placed on the plate.

Paper napkins are perfectly correct for family meals. If you prefer cloth napkins, you may wish to conserve your laundry by using napkin rings. Each member of the family has his or her own ring, marked so that he can recognize it, either by color or with a small initial. Napkins are then folded at the end of the meal and put back in the ring, which is removed from the table until the next meal. Napkins should be changed after two or three meals—of course if they are badly soiled they should not be used again until washed.

If this is your family practice, it is a good idea to explain to children that when they are guests in someone's home where napkin rings are used they would *not* put their napkins back in the ring after dinner.

Family Place Settings

Since no china or silver that will not be used need be placed on the table, the following settings must be reduced to fit your menu.

Family place setting.

BREAKFAST

In setting the breakfast table, you put out just those utensils that will be needed by each person.

A variety of cold cereals, milk, cream, sugar, salt and pepper and jams or jellies may be placed in the center of the table or on a convenient side table, but whoever is doing the cooking serves the hot food directly onto the plates and places them in front of those sitting at the table. If your table is large enough, a lazy susan or turntable is most convenient and makes each item easily accessible to everyone.

The setting is as follows:

Fork at the left of the plate

Knife at the right of the plate

Spoon for cereal at the right of the knife

Teaspoon for fruit or grapefruit spoon at the right of the cereal spoon

Napkins, in rings or not, at the left of the place setting

Coffee cups with spoons on the saucers or mugs at the right of each plate if the coffee is served from the kitchen. If it is served at the table, cups and saucers, or mugs, and coffeepot beside the person pouring.

Glass for milk or water to the right and above the spoons

Glass for juice to the right of the milk or water glass

Butter knife across the bread-and-butter plate, which is to the left and above the fork and which is completely optional at breakfast

LUNCH

The family lunch table is set in accordance with the food to be served. In the average household, no more than three courses are ever served for lunch, and even that number is most unusual.

The setting is as follows:

Meat fork at the left of the salad fork

On the right, a meat knife; and at the right of this knife, a soup or dessert spoon, if necessary

Butter plate and knife above the fork at the left

The dessert fork or spoon may be presented with the dessert plate if you prefer

Glass for a beverage above the knife

Napkin at the left of the place setting

DINNER

If the food is to be passed, the warm dinner plates are at each place on the table when the family sits down, or they are stacked in front of whoever is serving if the meal is served in this way. Some people prefer to serve the plates directly from the stove in order to avoid the use of extra platters and serving dishes. This is acceptable, but it should not be the only way dinner is served for it gives children no experience in being served or in passing food to the next person.

The table setting for dinner is similar to that for lunch:

At the left of the plate, the dinner fork.

At the right, the dinner knife next to the plate, then the soup spoon or the oyster fork or the dessert spoon (if necessary) on the outside.

Glass or goblet for a beverage at the right above the knife.

Butter plate to the left and above the fork, with the butter knife laid on it diagonally from the upper left to the lower right.

Salad plate at the left of the fork.

Napkin at the left of the setting.

Coffee mug or cup and saucer with a spoon at the right, if coffee is served with the meal.

THE MEALTIME TRAY

Although few people in the ordinary household are served breakfast on a tray, there are many occasions when a member of the family is ill and must remain in bed for his meals. An attractive tray with a flower in a little vase or with a brightly colored napkin and tray cloth can do much to aid a lagging appetite and a sagging spirit. Also, dinner is frequently eaten from a tray taken to the living room or den when a favorite television program is in progress.

For all meals, the tray is covered with a tray cloth, a doily or a place mat of some sort. The setting is the same as the individual place setting at the table insofar as space permits. Because of lack of room, the dessert plate and the coffee cup and saucer are usually brought when the main meal is finished. The dinner plate should be heated. A piece of foil laid over the food will keep it warm when the tray is carried to its destination.

Individual breakfast sets for trays were often given as wedding presents but today are more often purchased for someone confined to bed. They generally include an egg cup, a cereal bowl, two or three plates and a cover, a coffee cup and saucer, sugar bowl, cream pitcher and small coffee pot. They come in colorful patterns or lovely solid colors and by the very charm of their appearance make the morning more cheerful.

THE BARBECUE TABLE

Since the setting is informal, the barbecue table is one of two places (the other being a picnic) where disposable plates, cups and utensils are not only appropriate but also a very good idea.

Because the nature of a barbecue is festive, table settings should be bright and cheerful. Centerpieces can be fresh flowers arranged in unusual containers, such as copper kettles or earthenware jugs. Also on the table should be a basket holding additional paper napkins, since much barbecued food is eaten, in part at least, with the hands. Since finger bowls would seem ridiculous in such an informal setting, little packets of premoistened hand wipes are a thoughtful addition to the table. They may be put at each guest's place before the meal begins, or distributed at the end, passed in a small basket.

For an evening barbecue, there should be plenty of light, both for the chef to see what he or she is cooking and for guests to be able to maneuver easily. Hurricane candles on the table, perhaps in addition to citronella candles, which help keep insects at bay, are a good addition to floodlights directed into the trees or colorful paper lanterns strung along the patio or deck.

If the evening becomes cool, the hosts should think about inviting everyone inside for coffee, which the hostess would pour from a prepared tray in the living room.

THE PICNIC TABLE

Picnics provide the opportunity to be as whimsical as you wish whether the picnic table is a folding table set up in a parking lot for a tailgate party or an honest-to-goodness redwood table in the woods. Checkered cloths and paperware as well as a formal cloth and crystal and silver set the mood for your picnic. Utensils and plates must be planned around the menu. If the picnic consists of finger foods, little flatware is needed. When the menu is pheasant under glass, the full range of cutlery is required. Depending on how much can be carried safely, even vases and fresh flowers can be transported to the picnic site for a centerpiece to the meal. Because ingenuity is the guiding rule, there are no others—picnics are exempt from guidelines governing formal or informal dining experiences.

THE OPEN-HOUSE REFRESHMENT TABLE

This table should be set to accommodate a steady stream of "customers," conveniently placed in the center of a room, preferably, or against a wall if necessary. A pretty tablecloth, cocktail napkins and small plates are usually all that need be set on the table, along with chafing dishes, platters and plates of whatever you are serving. A centerpiece helps set the mood; a small, decorated tree or a basket of bright ornaments for a Christmas party; a carved pumpkin for a Halloween party.

It is a good idea to provide a waste receptacle on or near the table for used toothpicks, and to be sure that each food has its own serving utensil—knives for each cheese on a cheese tray; small scissors for snipping bunches of grapes; a spreader for a layered dip.

Because the refreshment table at an open house is a popular place and guests tend to linger at the table, it is a good idea to place beverages and glasses at another location. If they are on the same table as the food, crowd management becomes impossible and congestion is inevitable.

CARD PARTY REFRESHMENT TABLE

The kinds of refreshments you offer your card-playing guests depends, of course, on the time of day and whether you wish to serve before, during or after play. It is often simplest to set a small buffet on the dining room table, whatever the menu, so that guests may help themselves and be seated at the card tables to eat. It is unnecessary to set card tables with linens for a small refreshment. When everyone is finished, it is a good idea to wipe the tables before play begins or resumes. It is also a good idea to provide coasters at each table, since most guests will wish to continue drinking beverages as they play.

When your offering is more elaborate and if your dining table can accommodate all your guests, you may of course set it with a tablecloth or place mats and serve at this table. This is appropriate whether your refreshments are a full lunch, a dessert and coffee or a midnight snack.

4

Dining How To's:

Tricky Foods, Mealtime Dilemmas and the Etiquette of Eating

Asparagus, some connoisseurs will tell you, is definitely a finger food. Imagine the consternation the guest at a formal dinner feels, after trusting this advice, when faced with asparagus coated in Hollandaise sauce. Imagine the covert glances he would receive if he were to indeed pluck a spear with his fingers, throw his head back, and toss the sauce-laden vegetable into his mouth, dripping a bit of Hollandaise on the tablecloth and down his pleated shirt front in the process. Always remember that the standard advice on how to eat particular foods depends in part on how they are served.

Diners are often confronted with situations that require a moment's thought, whether they be which utensil to use for what, what to do with one's napkin at the conclusion of a meal, or how to remove something unwanted from one's mouth gracefully. When uncertain, glance at what the hostess or other guests are doing for a clue as to how to proceed. Knowing what to do and how to do it gives you the confidence to act as though managing an escargots tong or being served from a silver platter is an everyday experience—even the very first time.

FROM APPLES TO ZITI

Although the basic etiquette for eating all foods is that they be transported to the mouth in manageable, bite-sized pieces, there are several tips for certain courses and for specific foods that require dexterity in handling. When presented with something you have never eaten before, what you do depends on the company you are in. When among friends, there is nothing embarrassing about saying, "I've never had escargots before. Show me how to eat them!" When at a formal function or among strangers, however, you may not want to admit to this. In this case, it is best to delay beginning, by having a sip of water or wine, and watch what several others are doing first and then follow along.

Apples and Pears

These two fruits are quartered, with a knife. The core is then cut away from each quarter, and the fruit is eaten with the fingers. Those who do not like the skin should pare each quarter separately. When pears are very juicy, they must be cut with the knife and eaten with the fork. *See also Fruit, Fresh.*

Apricots

See Cherries, Apricots and Plums

Artichokes

Whole artichokes are always eaten with the fingers. Beginning at the outside pull off one leaf at a time while holding the artichoke steady with your other hand. Dip the base of the leaf, which is the softer, meaty end of it, into the sauce provided: melted butter, Hollandaise sauce, or if the artichoke is served cold, mayonnaise. Then place the leaf between your teeth and pull it forward. The leaves closer to the center will have a greater edible portion than those at the outside. Place the inedible portion of each leaf neatly on the side of your plate.

When the leaves are all consumed and you reach the center of the artichoke, scrape away the thistlelike part with your knife. This fuzzy portion is inedible and is called the "choke." Place this along the side of your plate with the leaves. The remaining part of the artichoke is the heart, or bottom. Cut this into bite-sized pieces with a knife and fork and dip the pieces into the melted butter before eating.

ASPARAGUS

By reputation this is a finger food, but that depends on how it has been cooked. When it is prepared al dente so that the stalks are firm, and any sauce is only on the tips, you may pick it up with your fingers, one stalk at a time, and eat it from the tip to the opposite end. When the stalks are covered in sauce or are limp, then cut them with your fork or fork and knife and eat them in small pieces. All hard ends should be cut off asparagus before it is served. If this has not been done, do not attempt to eat the ends. If you can't cut them, you can't chew them. Cut or eat the spears to the point at which they cease to be tender and leave the remainder neatly on your plate.

A finger food until all the leaves are eaten, an artichoke may be held near the base with one hand. Pull leaves, beginning at the outside, one by one. Used leaves are placed neatly around the edge of the plate.

AVOCADOS

When avocado slices are served, they are cut and eaten with a fork. When avacados are served in halves, hold the shell to steady it with one hand and eat the fruit with a spoon. Leave the empty shell, which is inedible, on the plate. When a salad or other mixture is served in an avocado shell, it is permissible to hold the shell lightly with one hand while eating the contents with a fork held in the other hand. As with the remains of half an avocado, leave the shell on the plate, placing your fork on the plate as well between bites and when finished, not in the shell.

BACON

Breakfast bacon should be eaten with a fork when it is limp. When it is dry and crisp, so that it scatters into fragments when broken by the fork, fingers are permitted.

BANANAS

This fruit may be peeled halfway down and eaten bite by bite at the family table, but when dining out it is better to peel the skin all the way off, lay the fruit on your plate, cut it in slices, and eat it with a fork.

BARBECUED MEATS

By definition a barbecue is informal, so eating barbecued foods is done informally. When ribs, chops, chicken pieces, hamburgers and hot dogs are served, fingers are used instead of utensils. Naturally, steak, fish and other meats served in larger portions normally eaten with a fork are still eaten with a fork.

BERRIES

Berries are usually hulled or stemmed ahead of time, served with cream and sugar, and eaten with a spoon. When especially fine and freshly picked, strawberries are often served with their hulls on and sugar placed at one side of each person's plate. The hull of each berry is held in the fingers, and the fruit is dipped in the sugar and then eaten. The hull should then be placed on the side of the plate.

BOUILLABAISSE

Bouillabaisse is a fish stew often containing at least two types of fish. To be enjoyed to its fullest it requires the assistance of a variety of utensils, from soup spoons to seafood forks, knives, and often shellfish crackers. It is to be hoped that a large bowl is placed on the table for shells. If not, then empty shells should be placed on the plate under the soup bowl.

BREAD AND BUTTER

Bread should always be broken with the fingers into moderate-sized pieces—but not necessarily single-mouthful bits—before being eaten. To butter it, hold a piece on the edge of the bread-and-butter plate, or the place plate, and with a butter knife, spread enough butter on it for a mouthful or two at a time. If there is no butter knife, use any other knife you find available.

Although the general rule is that an entire piece of bread or a whole roll is never buttered at once, there are always common-sense exceptions. For example, hot biscuits or toast can of course be buttered all over immediately, since they are most delicious when the butter is quickly and thoroughly melted. Bread should never, however, be held flat on the palm and buttered with the hand held in the air.

Hot, buttered garlic bread served in many restaurants is usually brought to the table in a basket, sometimes sliced, sometimes not. If it is sliced, each diner takes a piece, puts it on his own plate, and passes the basket in a counterclockwise direction. If it is not already sliced, the diner in front of whom the basket is placed helps him- or herself by breaking off an individual-serving sized piece and then passes the basket on to the next person who also breaks off his own piece of bread.

Many elegant restaurants serve hot breads or a variety of breads, such as zucchini or carrot bread or specialities like hot corn bread sticks, instructing waiters to continually offer bread to diners. In these cases, there is no bread basket on the table. Rather the waiter stands to the left of each diner, and with tongs, places a slice or piece of each on every diner's plate. When he sees that the bread is finished, he returns to that diner or table and offers more. This kind of service ensures that the bread is indeed fresh and hot.

See also Butter.

BREAD, FLAT OR FRIED

Many Indian and Middle Eastern restaurants serve breads that have been fried or baked flat, such as *boori*, an Indian bread, or pita bread. These breads are brought whole to the table on plates or flat baskets. Break pieces off with your fingers and transfer a piece of bread to your plate to eat. It is polite to pass the plate or basket to others at the table rather than breaking off several pieces with your fingers.

BREAD, ROUND LOAF, SERVED ON CUTTING BOARD

Some restaurants present an entire round loaf of bread on a cutting board for you to slice yourself. This should be cut not like a round cake in wedges, but in slices. Starting at one side, thinly slice the crust off, and then slice toward the center.

BREADS AND BREAKFAST PASTRIES

Danish pastry or sticky buns should be cut in half or in quarters with a knife and eaten with the fingers, if not too sticky, or with a fork.

English muffins may be buttered a half at a time and jelly, honey or marmalade—after being put on your plate first—

added to one half at a time with your knife. They may then be cut in half again and eaten with the fingers.

Muffins should be cut in half either vertically or horizontally and buttered, one half at a time.

Popovers are opened and buttered, and then eaten in small pieces.

BUTTER

Every sort of bread, biscuit, toast and also hot griddle cakes and corn on the cob are buttered with a knife. But corn that has been cut off the cob, or rice, or potato— or anything else on your dinner plate—has seasoning or butter mixed in it with a fork.

When serving butter at the table, you may cut it in small squares and arrange it on a plate or you may serve it as a quarter of a pound, the way it is commonly sold. When pats are served, diners should lift them with the utensil provided (most often a butter knife or small fork) and transfer them to their own plates. When butter is served as a block, a pat is cut from one end and transferred to one's bread-and-butter plate or dinner plate. If there is no accompanying utensil, the butter is transferred with the diner's own clean knife. When butter is presented in a tub, the diner scoops a portion with her own knife or butter knife and places it on her bread-and-butter plate or dinner plate.

In a restaurant, when butter is offered in individually wrapped squares, you should open the wrapper and use your knife to push the square onto your plate, or butter plate, if there is one, folding the buttery side of the wrapper in and placing it on the edge of the plate, never on the tablecloth.

CAKE, LAYER

Slices of layer cake should be placed on their side on the dessert plate, not standing up. As with other foods, cake is presented to the diner as it would be eaten, and it is almost impossible to cut cake with a fork neatly and in bite sizes when it is standing up. If for some reason you are given a piece of cake in an upright position, turn it on its side using your dessert fork and spoon, or if there is no dessert spoon, whatever other utensil remains at your place. If all utensils have been cleared from the table, then do the best you can with your fork and even the fingers of your other hand.

See also Desserts, on how to eat cake à la mode.

CANDY AND PETITS FOURS

When candy, petits fours, mints or candied fruits are presented in pleated paper wrappers or cups, you should lift them from the serving dish in the paper, transferring them to your plate and eating them from there. Do not leave the paper on the serving plate.

CANTALOUPES AND OTHER MELONS

These fruits when served in halves or quarters and cut lengthwise are eaten with a spoon. When served in precut pieces, as in a fruit salad, they are eaten with a fork.

CAVIAR

Caviar is best served in a crystal bowl on a bed of cracked ice. When it is passed to you, or when it is presented on a cocktail buffet table, use the spoon with which it is presented to place a teaspoon on your plate. Using your own knife or spoon, then place small amounts on toast triangles, which may be buttered or not. If chopped egg, minced onions or sour cream is served with caviar, one or more of these toppings is spooned, sparingly, on top of the caviar.

CHEESE

Cheese, when served as an hors d'oeuvre, is cut or spread on a cracker with a knife. A separate knife should be provided for each cheese to prevent flavors from mixing.

When cheese is served with fruit for dessert, it is cut with a knife, placed on the plate with the fruit, which is also cut with a knife, and eaten by fork together with the fruit. Neither is ever picked up with the fingers.

CHERRIES, APRICOTS AND PLUMS

All of these fruits are eaten with the fingers. The pit of the fruit should be made as clean as possible in your mouth and then dropped into your almost closed, cupped hand and then to your plate. Plums and apricots are held in your fingers and eaten as close to the pit as possible. When you remove a pit with your fingers, you should do it with your thumb underneath and your first two fingers across your mouth, and not with your fingertips pointing into your mouth. If you prefer, pits can be pushed forward with the tongue onto a spoon and then dropped onto a plate.

CHERRY TOMATOES

Except when served in a salad or other dish, cherry tomatoes are eaten with the fingers. And they *squirt!* The best thing to do is to try and select one small enough to be put in your mouth whole. Even then, close your lips tightly before chewing. If you must bite into a larger one, make a little break in the skin with your front teeth before biting it in half. When served whole in a salad or other dish, cherry tomatoes are cut, carefully, with a knife and fork and eaten with the fork.

CHICKEN AND OTHER SMALL FOWL

At a formal dinner, no part of a bird is picked up with the fingers. However, among family and friends and in family style or informal restaurants, it is permissible to eat it as follows:

The main body of the bird is not eaten with the fingers. You cut off as much meat as you can and leave the rest on your plate. To eat the small bones, such as joints or wings, or the second joint of a squab, you hold the piece of bone with meat on it up to your mouth and eat it clean. Larger joints, too, such as the drumstick of a roast chicken, may be picked up after the first few easily cut off pieces have been eaten.

CHOPS

At a dinner party or in a formal restaurant, lamb chops must be eaten with knife and fork. The center, or "eye," of the chop is cut off the bone, and cut into two or three pieces. If the chop has a frilled paper "skirt" around the end of the bone, you may hold that in your hand and cut the tasty meat from the side of the bone. If there is no "skirt" you must do the best you can with your knife and fork. At the family table or in an informal group of friends, the center may be cut out and eaten with the fork, and the bone picked up and eaten clean with the teeth. This is permissible, too, with veal or pork chops, but only when they are broiled or otherwise served without sauce. When picking up a chop with your fingers, hold it with one hand only. If it is too big to hold with only one hand, it is too big to pick up.

CLAMS AND OYSTERS ON THE HALF SHELL

Clams and oysters on the half shell are generally served on cracked ice and arranged around a container of cocktail sauce. Hold the shell with the fingers of your left hand and hold the shellfish fork (or smallest fork provided) with the right hand. Spear the clam or oyster with the fork, dip it into sauce, and eat it with one bite. If a part of the clam or oyster sticks to the shell, use your fork to separate it from the shell. As an option, you may take a little of the sauce on your fork and drop it onto the clam, or if you prefer no sauce, you may squeeze a little lemon onto it before eating it.

If oyster crackers are served they may be crumbled up in the fingers and mixed into the sauce. Horseradish, too, is mixed into the sauce, or a drop may be put directly onto the shellfish if you like a hot taste.

When raw clams or oysters are ordered at a clam bar or eaten at a picnic, you may pick up the shell with the fingers and suck the clam or oyster and its juice right off the shell.

CLAMS, STEAMED

Steamed clams should be open at least halfway. If they aren't, don't eat them. Open the shell fully, holding it with your left hand, and pull out the clam with your fingers, if the setting is informal, or with a seafood fork, if it is more formal. If the clam is a true steamer, slip the skin off the neck with your fingers and put it aside. Dip steamed clams into melted butter or broth and eat them in one bite. Empty shells are placed in a bowl provided for that purpose, or around the edge of your plate if there is no bowl. It is permissible, if your host or hostess does so in a more formal setting, or just because you want to when the occasion is casual, to drink any broth provided for dipping after the clams are finished.

COCKTAIL TRIMMINGS

If you want to eat the olives, cherries or onions served in cocktails, by all means do so. If they are served on a toothpick or cocktail pick, simply remove them from the drink and enjoy them. If there is no pick, drink enough of the cocktail so that you will not wet your fingers, and lift out the olive or cherry and eat it in your fingers. Slices of oranges in old-fashioneds are not usually eaten as it is too messy to chew the pulp off the rind.

CONDIMENTS

When a relish or condiment tray is present, put your choices from it on your butter plate. If there is no butter plate, then place them on your salad plate or on the side of whatever plate is in front of you. Never take even a single olive directly from the condiment tray to your mouth—always place it first on a plate, and then pass the condiment tray to the person next to you.

When the condiment is cranberry sauce or relish, it should be eaten by lifting it onto the fork and either eating it as a separate mouthful or by taking some of it with a small piece of meat on the tips of the tines.

CORN ON THE COB

Corn should be cut from the cob and eaten with a fork at formal dinners. At all other occasions, however, it is picked up with the hands. Perhaps the only directions to be given for this vegetable are to attack it with as little ferocity as possible, and to eat it as neatly as possible. If melted butter has not been added in the kitchen, take pats of butter from the butter plate and place them on your dinner plate. Butter and season only a few rows of the corn at a time, repeating this process until the corn is finished.

CRABS, SOFTSHELL

Usually the entire crab can be eaten. When served as a sandwich, cut the sandwich into reasonable pieces, pick it up with the fingers, and eat. When served separately, the crabs should be cut with a knife and fork down the middle and then into bite-sized sections. The legs can be eaten as part of the crab, if it is truly a soft shell. Inedible hard parts should be placed on the side of your plate.

CRACKERS OR CROUTONS WITH SOUP

Crackers or croutons are scattered on soup after it has been ladled into the plate to be served. If passed, oyster crackers, as well as any others, are transferred from the serving plate to one's bread-and-butter plate and dropped from there, two or three pieces at a time, into the soup. Larger soda crackers are broken and then scattered over the soup a few pieces at a time. Croutons are passed in a dish with a small serving spoon so that each person may scatter a spoonful or more over his soup directly from the serving dish, making sure that the spoon does not actually touch the soup.

CRANBERRY SAUCE

See Condiments.

CREAM PUFFS

See Dessert.

CRUDITÉS

When fresh vegetables and dip are offered, only dip the vegetable once, never after taking a bite of the vegetable. If raw vegetables are passed as a relish at the table, place them on your bread-and-butter plate, or, if there isn't one, on your salad plate or on the edge of whatever plate is in front of you. Never transfer a relish directly from the serving plate to your mouth.

DANISH PASTRIES

See Breads and Breakfast Pastries.

DESSERT

Dessert may be eaten with spoon or fork or both. Stewed fruit is held in place with the spoon and cut and eaten with the fork or it may be cut with the edge of a spoon and eaten with it. Peaches or other very juicy fruits are peeled and then eaten with knife and fork, but dry fruits, such as apples, may be cut and eaten with the fingers, unless they are served with cheese, in which case they are cut and eaten with the fork.

Cake and pie are eaten with a fork; if it is "à la mode," the spoon is also used. Ice cream is generally eaten with a spoon,

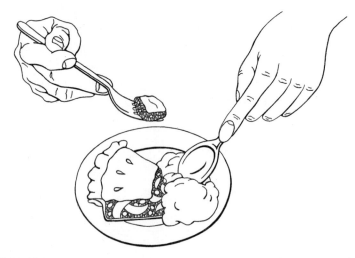

Pie and cake à la mode are eaten with a dessert fork and spoon. The spoon is used to cut and place a bite of cake or pie and a bite of ice cream on the fork, which is held in the right hand and used to eat the dessert.

but when accompanied by cake, either the spoon alone or both the spoon and fork may be used.

Pastries, such as cream puffs and Napoleons, are held with the dessert spoon and cut and eaten with the dessert fork. Bite sized pastries may be picked up with the fingers. The general rule is that if you cannot eat something, no matter what it is, without getting it all over your fingers or face, you must use a fork, and when necessary, a spoon or a knife also.

ENGLISH MUFFINS

See Breads and Breakfast Pastries.

ESCARGOTS

See Snails (Escargots).

FETTUCCINI

See Spaghetti, Linguini and Fettuccini.

FISH

Most often, fish is served in filet form and is eaten with a fish fork and fish knife, or in their absence, any knife and fork that is in front of you. In a restaurant, when you are served a fish that is not fileted, simply ask the waiter to filet it for you, unless you are a whiz at this yourself. When you have no choice but to do it yourself, insert the tip of your knife under the backbone of the fish and slide the knife under the skeleton, lifting it with the knife and placing it on the side of your plate. If the fish has a head, cut the head off before you filet the fish.

If you find small bones in your mouth when eating fish, push them to the front of your mouth with your tongue and then onto your fork, removing them to the side of your plate.

FONDUE

Cheese fondue is served in a fondue pot that is kept warm by Sterno heat or electric heat. It is accompanied by a bowl of bite-sized squares of French bread. A piece of bread is speared on a long fondue fork and dipped into the hot cheese. When sufficiently coated, it is withdrawn, held over the pot for a moment to drip, and is removed from the fondue fork with the tines of the dinner fork onto the dinner plate. The fondue fork is put down and the bread is eaten with the dinner fork.

Meat fondue, in which pieces of meat on the fondue fork are plunged into very hot oil to cook, is eaten much the same way. A bowl of raw meat is passed to each diner, who takes several pieces and places them on his dinner plate. A selection of sauces is also passed, and diners select some or all and place a spoonful of each around their dinner plate. Diners firmly spear a piece of raw meat with their long fondue forks and place them in the pot. Ideally, unless the pot is very large, there are no more than four to six diners per pot and therefore no more than four to six fondue forks holding meat to cook in each pot.

Each diner removes the cooked meat to his dinner plate to let it cool. It is then cut into smaller pieces with the dinner fork and knife, dipped into a choice of fondue sauces, and eaten while the next piece of meat is sizzling in the pot on the end of the fondue fork.

FOOD PREPARED TABLESIDE

Certain dishes in restaurants may be prepared at tableside by the captain and/or waiter. It could be a pasta tossed in a sauce, a dessert of flambéed bananas, or the entire entrée is cooked at the table, as at a Japanese steakhouse. Your attention is appreciated during these demonstrations, and your exclamations of pleasure as well. You do not participate, and when flame is used, you should remain seated.

FOWL

See Chicken and Other Small Fowl.

FRENCH FRIES

See Potatoes.

FRENCH ONION SOUP

See Soups with Toppings.

FROGS' LEGS

Frogs' legs may be eaten with the fingers or with a knife and fork, with the inedible portions moved to the side of the plate with the knife and fork.

FRUIT, FRESH

Seasonal fresh fruit may be served as dessert or as a course before the dessert course. The equipment for eating raw fruit at the table consists of a sharp-bladed fruit knife, a fork and a finger bowl. In a restaurant, when no knife is given you, it is

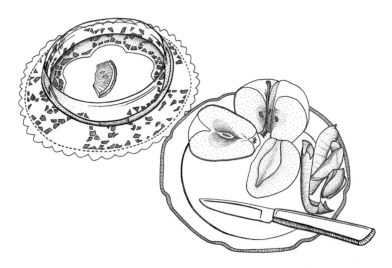

Large fruits are quartered first with a sharp fruit knife and then peeled, if desired, before being eaten. The discarded peel and any seeds are moved to the side of the plate.

proper to ask for one. *See also the entries for individual fruits for additional information.*

Fruit, Stewed

Stewed prunes, cherries, etc. are eaten with a spoon. The fruit is put into the mouth whole, and the fruit is eaten off the pit before the pit is dropped directly onto the spoon from the lips and deposited on the edge of the plate or saucer.

Garnishes

Often food is decorated with a garnish, whether fresh parsley sprigs or lemon rind. These garnishes may be eaten or not, depending on your personal preference. Parsley is useful as a natural breath deodorizer, which is why it is often served with spicy, garlic or onion-laden dishes. If you elect not to consume a garnish, just move it to the side of your plate.

GAZPACHO

See Soups with Toppings.

GRAPEFRUIT

Grapefruit should be served with the seeds removed and with each section precut and loosened. The rind and any seeds should be left on the plate.

GRAPES

These should never be pulled off the bunch one at a time. Choose a branch with several grapes on it and break it off, or if scissors are provided, cut the bunch off close to the main stem.

Seedless grapes are no problem to eat at all, since the entire fruit, skin and all, is eaten and there are no seeds to worry about.

Grapes with seeds can be eaten in one of two ways. First, a grape may be laid on its side, held with the fingers of one hand and cut in the center with the point of a knife, which also lifts and removes the seeds.

The alternative is put the grapes in your mouth whole and then to deposit the seeds into your fingers and place them on your plate as elegantly as possible after eating the fruit.

Concord or garden grapes with difficult-to-digest skin should be pressed between your lips and against your almost-closed teeth so that the juice and pulp will be drawn into your mouth and the skin left to be discarded.

GRAVIES AND SAUCES

You may sop bread in gravy, but it must be done properly—by putting a small piece down on the gravy and then eating it with your fork as though it were any other helping on your plate. You may put it into your mouth "continental" style, with the tines pointed down as they were when you sopped up the gravy. Sauce may also be finished in this way.

Hors D'Oeuvres

When hors d'oeuvres are hot, it is wise to wait a few moments until they cool before putting them in your mouth. They can do serious damage to the inside of your mouth if popped in while still burning hot.

If toothpicks are offered, spear the hors d'oeuvre, put it in your mouth and then place the used toothpick on a plate or receptacle put out for that purpose, or hold it in your napkin until you can find a waste basket. Do not ever put a used tooth-pick back on the serving tray.

When appetizers have their own remnants, such as Alaska king crab claws, or shrimp tails, hold them in a paper napkin until such time as you can dispose of them.

Do not discard toothpicks, napkins, uneaten appetizers or remnants in ashtrays. It is unattractive and potentially haz-ardous should a lighted cigarette set fire to a paper napkin.

Kiwis

This tart-sweet fruit with a bristlelike fuzzy skin is peeled and then sliced like a tomato. If presented with an unpeeled kiwi, use a sharp paring knife to peel away the outer skin, which is inedible, and then slice the kiwi crosswise, further cutting it into bite sized pieces and eating it with a fork. There is no need to remove the seeds as they are edible.

Lamb Chops

See Chops.

Lasagna

See Ziti, Lasagna and Layered Pasta.

LAYER CAKE

See Cake, Layer.

LEMONS

Fruits that are not frequently eaten on their own, lemons are often used as a accompaniment or garnish to other dishes. When serving a lemon, cut it in wedges, slices, quarters or halves, depending on its end use, removing as many seeds as are visible.

LINGUINI

See Spaghetti, Linguini and Fettuccini.

LOBSTER

Lobster claws should be cracked at all points, the tail split in half and the dead man or intestines removed before the lobster is served. Guests should be provided with individual nutcrackers or shellfish crackers to finish the process as well as with seafood forks for extracting the lobster meat. The cracking of claws at the table should be done slowly so that the juice does not squirt when the shell breaks. Hold the lobster steady with one hand and, holding the nutcracker in your other hand, twist off the claws from the body and place them on the side of your plate. Crack each claw and pull out the meat. The meat is removed from the large claw ends and from each joint with a pick or with a shellfish fork. The tail meat is pulled out of the shell in two solid pieces—one side at a time. It is then cut into bite-sized pieces with a knife or the side of a dinner fork, and dipped into melted butter if hot, or mayonnaise if cold. The red roe and the green "fat" or "tamale" are edible and delectable to some, who put a small bit of one or both on the fork with each bite of lobster meat. Real lobster-lovers get an additional morsel out of the legs by breaking off one at a time, putting them into

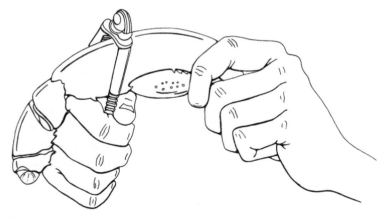

Lobster and crab claws are held in one hand and a nutcracker held in the other hand. Squeeze the nutcracker along the shell of the claw until it cracks open enough for the meat to be extracted with a fork.

the mouth and biting up the shell, squeezing the meat out of the broken end.

A large bowl or platter should be provided for discarded, empty shells.

Properly, a big paper napkin or plastic bib is provided for the lobster-eater. Wear it, since the work involved in eating a lobster often produces a few squirts and splashes as shells are cracked. Finger bowls with hot water and lemon slices should be put at the side of each place as soon as people are finished eating. These are carried away after the dinner plates have been removed.

Melon

See Cantaloupes and Other Melons.

Mints

See Candy and Petit Fours.

Muffins

See Breads and Breakfast Pastries.

MUSSELS

Mussels, like some steamed clams, may be served in their shells in the broth in which they are steamed, this is generally called *moules marinieres*. The mussel may be removed from its shell with a fork, then dipped into the sauce and eaten in one bite. Depending on the company you are keeping and the informality of the location, it is permissible to pick up the shell, scooping a little of the juice with it, and suck the mussel and juice directly off the shell. Empty shells are placed in a bowl or plate, which should always be provided for them. The juice or broth remaining in the bowl may be eaten with a spoon, or you may sop it up with pieces of roll or French bread speared on the tines of your fork.

NAPOLEANS

See Dessert.

NECTARINES

This fruit is halved and the pit is removed, then the fruit is halved again. It may or may not be peeled, according to personal preference.

OLIVES

Eat olives with your fingers when they are served as a relish. If there are stones, bite off the meat of the olive but don't actually "clean" the stone. Remove the stone from your mouth with your fingers, or by pushing it with your tongue onto a spoon. Bite a large, stuffed olive in half. Put only a very small one in your mouth whole. When the olive is in a salad, eat it with your fork, not your fingers.

ONION SOUP, FRENCH

See Soups with Toppings.

ORANGES AND TANGERINES

These citrus fruits may be eaten by slicing the two ends of the rind off first and then cutting the peel off in vertical strips. If the peel is thick and loose, it can be pulled off with the fingers. Tangerines can be pulled apart into small sections before eating, while oranges are more easily cut with a knife. Seeds should be taken out from the center with the tip of the knife and sections eaten with the fingers. If there is fiber around the peeled orange or tangerine, it may be removed with the fingers. Any remaining fiber and seeds can be removed from the mouth neatly with the thumb and first two fingers (fingers above and thumb underneath).

ORIENTAL FOODS

Those familiar and comfortable with chopsticks should use them when they are offered. Food is usually served in small pieces so that it does not need to be cut. When larger pieces are served, however, the chopsticks, held together, are used to "chop" or cut the piece in half or to bite-size when possible. Large pieces of meat can be picked up with the chopsticks and eaten by biting off small mouthfuls one at a time.

If individual dipping sauces are provided, food is dipped into the dish—the sauce is not poured over the food, as gravy would be ladled onto mashed potatoes. Each bite is held with the chopsticks, dipped and raised to the mouth.

Rice is almost impossible to grasp in mouthfuls and raise from plate to mouth. Because of this, the individual rice bowl is raised to a point just under the chin and the chopsticks are used to scoop rice into the mouth. If a fork is used, then the rice bowl is left on the table and a forkful at a time is brought to the mouth.

Dumplings and other small, stuffed whole items often found on an appetizer platter are taken whole with the chopsticks and raised to the mouth. If they are slightly too big to put entirely in the mouth, they may be bitten in half. This can be tricky for the uninitiated, since a firm grasp must be kept on the part that is not being eaten.

Soup is eaten with the flat spoon provided. Even though served in a cup, it usually is not drunk from the cup.

Chinese tea, which is provided by the pot, is poured by whoever is closest to it, with each diner passing his or her cup to the one pouring. A milk or cream pitcher is rarely ever set on a table in an Oriental restaurant—the expectation is that you add nothing but perhaps sugar to your tea. If you must have milk, however, you certainly may ask your waiter to bring it to you. In Japanese restaurants a green tea is often served. This mild tea is not accompanied by sugar or milk.

When large platters are placed on the table, a serving spoon is usually provided to accompany each and diners serve themselves from the platters, leaving the serving spoon on the platter. If no spoon is provided, chopsticks may be used to transfer food from plate to platter, but they must be turned around so that the larger end, the one that has not been in the mouth, is used.

OYSTERS ON THE HALF SHELL

See Clams and Oysters on the Half Shell.

PAPAYAS AND POMEGRANATES

These tropical fruits are served halved or quartered with the seeds removed. The fruit is scooped from its shell with a spoon.

PASTA

See Spaghetti, Linguini and Fettuccini.

PASTA, LAYERED

See Ziti, Lasagna and Layered Pasta.

PEACHES

This fragrant, juicy fruit is cut to the pit, then broken in half and eaten. Since most people don't like the fuzzy skin of a peach, they are almost always peeled before eating.

PEARS

See Apples and Pears.

PEAS

Peas are perhaps one of the most difficult vegetables to capture and eat. You may use your knife as a pusher to get them onto your fork, *(see illustration page 157)* or you may use the tines of the fork to actually spear a few peas at a time.

PETITS FOURS

See Candy and Petits Fours.

PIE

A slice of pie is cut and eaten with the fork, with the assistance of the dessert spoon if the crust is difficult to cut with the fork alone. When cheese is served with apple pie, it may be lifted with the fork and spoon and placed on top of the pie to be cut and eaten with each bite. *See also Desserts for how to eat pie à la mode.*

PINEAPPLE

This prickly tropical fruit is sliced into round pieces, is peeled and served on a plate to be eaten with a dessert fork and spoon.

PITA BREAD

See Bread, Flat or Fried.

PIZZA

Pizza is cut into wedges with a knife or pizza cutter and served this way. Individual wedges may be picked up and eaten with the fingers. Some pizza lovers prefer to fold the pizza in at the center to keep edges from hanging outward and dripping before lifting it to their mouths. Pizza may also be cut into bite-sized pieces with a knife and fork and eaten with a fork.

PLUMS

See Cherries, Apricots and Plums.

POMEGRANATES

See Papayas and Pomegranates.

POPOVERS

See Breads and Breakfast Pastries.

PORK CHOPS

See Chops.

POTATOES

There are many different ways to eat potatoes. Baked potato, whether white or sweet, can be broken in half with the fingers after cutting a slit with a knife first. With a fork scoop all the inside of the potato onto the plate, then, if you like, mix butter, salt and pepper into it.

Another way to eat baked potato is to break it in half with the fingers and lay both halves, skin down, on the plate. If you enjoy butter or sour cream you can mix a little butter into part of one half with a fork and eat that. Then mix a little more, and so on, eating it out of the skin without turning it onto the plate.

A third way—for those who like to eat the skin as well as the inside—is to cut the baked potato in half and then cut the halves into pieces, a few at a time. If you wish to eat the skins separately, scrape the inside part onto your plate, put the skins on the side of the plate, and eat a small piece at a time. When baked potato is served in aluminum foil, put the foil to one side or on the butter plate.

When French fried potatoes accompany finger foods, such as hamburgers, hot dogs or other sandwiches, they may be eaten with the fingers. At other times they should be cut into reasonable lengths and eaten with a fork.

RELISHES

See Condiments.

SALAD

Cut large pieces of lettuce with a fork, or a fork and knife if they are particularly springy and difficult to cut with a fork only. Cut only one bite at a time—never attack your salad bowl or plate with your knife and fork and cut the entire plateful into small pieces at once.

Use your salad fork if the salad is served on a separate salad plate. If it is served on your entrée plate, eat it with your entrée fork.

When salad is served as a separate course between the entrée and dessert, it is often served with cheese and crackers. If you like, take small portions of one or two cheeses and put them on your salad plate, along with two or three crackers. The cheese is eaten with your fork, as you eat the salad, and the crackers with your fingers.

When an entrée salad is served with dressing on the side, it can be a very difficult to add salad dressing to a full bowl. With a chef's salad, spoon or pour a little dressing over the part of the salad you intend to eat first. Continue in this manner until you have lowered the height of the salad enough to reach the lettuce underneath. At this time, you may be able to mix the dressing throughout more easily.

SALT IN A SALTCELLAR

Although we are used to seeing salt shakers on the table today, some hostesses will set out saltcellars (tiny round silver or crystal containers). If there is no spoon in the saltcellar, use the tip of a clean knife to take some salt. If the saltcellar is for you alone, you may either use the tip of your knife or you may take a pinch with your fingers. If it is to be shared with others, do not ever use your fingers or a knife that is not clean.

Salt that is to be dipped into should be put on the bread-and-butter plate or on the rim of whatever plate is before you.

Please taste your food before salting it. You cannot possibly know how much salt was added during the preparation of the food until you taste it. You may find the taste to your liking without additional salt.

SANDWICHES

Sandwiches are usually eaten with the fingers. Club sandwiches and other thick sandwiches are best cut into small portions before being picked up and held tightly in the fingers of both hands. Sandwiches that are served open-faced and with gravy, such as hot turkey or roast beef sandwiches, are cut with a knife and fork and eaten with a fork.

SASHIMI

See Sushi and Sashimi.

SAUCES

See Gravies and Sauces.

SHISH KABOB

Except for shish kabob served as an hors d'oeuvre, you do not eat directly from the skewer. When shish kabob is served as a main course, lift the skewer with one hand and with the other, use your fork, beginning with the pieces at the bottom, to push and slide the meat and vegetables off the skewer and onto your plate. Place the now-emptied skewer on the edge of your plate, and with your knife and fork, cut the meat and vegetables into manageable pieces a bite at a time.

SHRIMP COCKTAIL

Shrimp as a first course can present one of the most difficult problems encountered by the diner. If not too impossibly large, each shrimp should be eaten in one bite. But when shrimp are of jumbo size, the diner has no alternative but to firmly grasp with one hand the cup in which they are served and cut the shrimp as neatly as possible with the edge of the fork. It is impractical to use a knife because the stemmed shrimp-cup will tip over unless held with one hand. If the saucer or plate under the shrimp cup is large enough, you might also remove a shrimp from the cup, place it on the saucer and cut it there with a knife and fork. At home the problem can be avoided by arranging the shrimp attractively on a small plate—where they can easily be cut with knife or fork—and I see no reason why restaurants should not do the same.

Shrimp cocktail is eaten with the smallest fork at your place. If there is a lemon wedge served with the shrimp, and you like the taste of lemon on shrimp, spear it with your fork and then, covering it with your other hand, squeeze it carefully over the shrimp. Some restaurants serve lemon wedges wrapped in cheesecloth so they do not squirt and the seeds do not drop out. You squeeze the lemon juice right through the cheesecloth. If sauce is served, you can dip your shrimp into the sauce, if it is your dish alone, or take some with a spoon and spoon it over the shrimp when the sauce dish is shared.

SNAILS (ESCARGOTS)

Snail shells are grasped with a special holder, in one hand, or with the fingers if no holder is provided. The meat is removed

Especially designed for holding snail shells, escargot tongs are held in one hand. The snail shell fits into the tongs and is held securely while the snail is extracted from the shell with a fork held in the other hand.

with a pick or oyster fork held in the other hand. The garlic butter that remains in the shells may be poured into the snail plate and sopped up with small pieces of French bread on the end of a fork and eaten with the fork.

SOUPS

Either clear soup or thick soup may be served in a cup with one handle or with handles on two sides. After taking a spoonful or two, you may pick up the cup if the soup is cool enough, and drink the remainder. Or you may continue to eat the soup with your soup spoon. Soups may also be served in soup bowls which are never picked up in the hand.

Clear soups are sometimes served in a shallow soup plate rather than in a cup. When the level of the soup is so low that you must tip the plate to avoid scraping the bottom noisily, lift the near edge with one hand and tip the plate away from you. Then the soup may be spooned away from you.

Soup cups, soup plates and bowls should be served with a saucer or plate beneath them. The spoon, when not in use or when the soup is finished, is laid on the saucer when a soup cup or bowl is used, but is left in the soup plate rather than on the dish under it.

Never leave spoon in cup or bowl.

Always place spoon on underplate.

Spoons should never be left in soup or dessert cups either between bites or when you are finished. They should be placed on the plate under the bowl or dish presented with the course instead.

SOUPS WITH TOPPINGS

Such soups as French onion, which is served with a crouton inside and cheese baked and bubbled on the top, requires two utensils for eating. The soup spoon is used to eat the soup, while a knife or even a fork is required to cut the cheese on the rim of the soup cup or dish so that it does not trail from bowl to mouth in a long string. Initially, when the bowl is full and there is danger of splashing, it is not incorrect to take a small amount of the cheese on the spoon and twist it around the bowl of the spoon, cutting it neatly at the edge with the fork or knife. This provides access to the soup underneath. The spoon may then be dipped into the bowl so a spoonful of soup is eaten with the cheese already on the spoon.

Soups such as gazpacho which have optional toppings are garnished before you begin eating. These toppings, which include croutons, chopped onions or peppers, are spooned from their serving dishes and sprinkled directly onto the soup. There is no need to place them first on a salad plate or bread-and-butter plate. The serving spoon should never touch the plate. Any serving spoons should then be placed or rested on the underplate, never left sticking out of the bowl or dish.

See also Crackers or Croutons with Soup.

SPAGHETTI, LINGUINI AND FETTUCCINI

Spaghetti seems to present a great challenge to diners, although there are three ways to eat it that are not difficult to

Spaghetti and other long pasta may be twirled around a fork resting on the bowl of a large spoon.

master. The first is simply to cut spaghetti, linguini, fettuccini or other long pasta into sections and eat it with a fork. The second is to take a few strands on your fork and twirl the spaghetti around the fork, holding the tines against the edge of your plate. The third is to hold the fork in one hand and a large, dessert-sized spoon in the other. Take a few strands of the pasta on the fork and place the tines against the bowl of the spoon, twirling the fork to wrap the spaghetti around itself as it turns.

If the latter two methods are used, the spaghetti should be twirled until there are no dangling ends. Bring the fork to your mouth. If ends do unwind themselves from around the fork, you must either suck them (quietly, please!) into your mouth, or bite them neatly, hoping they fall back onto your fork and do not drop to your chest or plate.

When pasta is served with the sauce ladled on top and not mixed in, you should mix it neatly, using a fork and spoon, before eating.

STICKY BUNS

See Breads and Breakfast Pastries.

STRAWBERRIES

See Berries.

SUSHI AND SASHIMI

Sushi is served in small pieces that may be eaten whole. If you're using a fork and the pieces are too large, you may cut them with the fork or with a fork and sharp knife. If eaten with chopsticks, the fish is picked up whole and eaten from the chopsticks, or the ends of the chopsticks may be used to cut the portions into smaller pieces. If you're using your fingers and the piece is large, you may bite it in half. When soy sauce is provided, one end of the sushi portions may be dipped into it and put in the mouth.

The small end of a pair of chopsticks is used for eating. Once used they never touch any communal bowl.

Sashimi, which is thinly sliced, boneless fish, is generally eaten with chopsticks.

If you are serving yourself from a serving platter of sushi or sashimi, you should turn your chopsticks around and pick up pieces.

TACOS AND TORTILLAS

Tacos and tortillas are meant to be eaten with the hands, since it is impossible to cut into the crisp shell with a knife and fork without having it crack and crumble. However, any filling that falls out should be eaten with a fork, not picked up with the hands.

TANGERINES

See Oranges and Tangerines.

TEA BAGS

A tea bag should never be served in a cup of tea. Preferably, tea is steeped in a pot and then poured into cups and served. Sometimes, however, a host or hostess will indeed bring you a cup with the tea bag floating inside. If this happens and the tea has reached the strength you enjoy, lift the bag from the cup with the spoon, hold it at the top of the cup while it drains and place it on the saucer under the cup. Do not wind the string around the spoon and squeeze the tea bag dry. When tea is served in mugs, a tea bag holder of some sort should be provided. If it is not, it is necessary to ask, "Where would you like me to put my tea bag?"

Many restaurants serve tea by bringing individual pots of hot water to the table for each tea drinker. Each pot is served on a saucer accompanied by one or more tea bags. Place the tea bag into the pot and allow the tea to steep. When the tea reaches the strength you enjoy, remove the tea bag and place it on the saucer.

TOMATOES, CHERRY

See Cherry Tomatoes.

WATERMELON

This delightful summer fruit is cut into large-sized pieces or slices and usually eaten with the fingers. If using a fork, remove the seeds with the tines and then cut the pieces with the side of the fork.

VEAL CHOPS

See Chops.

ZITI, LASAGNA AND LAYERED PASTA

Layered pasta dishes, such as ziti and lasagna, present their own unique eating problem when melted, stringy, mozzarella cheese stretches from the plate to the fork to the mouth with every bite. When this occurs, use your knife to cut portions and especially to cut through the cheese before attempting to eat a mouthful. This prevents the rather unattractive sight of strings of cheese hanging from your mouth and chin as you dine.

THE ETIQUETTE OF EATING

Knowing which leaves to pluck from the artichoke first and how to tackle a kiwi at a formal dinner table gives immeasurable confidence in every dining situation, but knowing how to eat gracefully adds the polish that will ensure that you are an attractive addition to any table.

From the Outside In: Managing Flatware

There should never be any question about which silver to use. *You always start with the utensil of each type that is farthest from the plate.* This question arises again and again, and the answer is always the same, with one exception. If the table is incorrectly set, and you realize that you cannot use the implement for the course that its position indicates, you must, naturally, choose the next one that is appropriate. For example, if the small shellfish fork has been put next to the plate, you would not use the dinner fork for the shrimp cocktail and leave the little fork for the main course, even though they were placed in that order. Otherwise you assume that the table is correctly set, and starting at the outside, you work your way with each course, toward the center.

When the menu calls for a dessert spoon and fork, they may be arranged at the top of the place setting before dinner begins. The American style places the spoon on top, with the handle of the spoon to the right and the handle of the fork to the left.

Dessert Spoon and Fork

The spoon and fork for the dessert course may be placed at the top of the place setting, American style, with the handle of the spoon to the right and the handle of the fork to the left or European style with both handles on the right. They are not used until dessert is served. If they are not placed above the service plate, a dessert spoon may be placed on the inside right of the place setting, between the knives and the soup spoon, or the dessert spoon and/or fork may be brought on the plate on which dessert is served.

How to Position Flatware When Pausing, When Passing Your Plate and When Finished

When you are pausing between bites but have not finished, simply place your knife and fork together toward the right side of your plate.

When at a dinner where the host or hostess is serving from

Flatware placed on the side of your plate in this position signals that you are finished with your meal and that your plate may be removed.

his or her place and you are passing your plate for a second helping, always leave the knife and fork on the plate and be sure they are positioned enough toward the center so that they will not topple off. You never put your used flatware on the tablecloth or place mat, nor do you sit, clutching your knife and fork in your fist, waiting for your plate to be passed back to you.

When you have finished the main course the knife and fork are placed beside each other on the dinner plate diagonally from upper left to lower right. The handles extend slightly over the edge of the plate. The dessert spoon or fork is placed in the same position. If dessert is served in a stemmed bowl or in a small, deep bowl, on another plate, the dessert spoon is put down on the plate when you are finished. If the bowl is shallow and wide, the spoon may be left in it, or on the plate below it, as you wish.

Do not clench your fists around your silverware.

Do hold your knife and fork in a relaxed manner, using your forefingers to guide both utensils, like this.

How to Hold Flatware

It is surprising how many people grip their eating utensils with their hands in a fist. It is much more comfortable to hold them lightly. The fork and spoon are held with the thumb and forefinger at a position on the fork that is comfortable, usually about three-quarters of the way up the handle. Your other three fingers then fit loosely and comfortably behind the handle, with the middle finger serving as a support from underneath.

When a fork is used to hold food in place so it can be cut by a knife, it is held about two-thirds of the way down the handle with the thumb applying pressure from the bottom and the forefinger applying pressure from the top. During this process, the knife is held about halfway down the handle with the thumb and middle finger, while the forefinger presses firmly on the top of the blade where it joins the handle.

This is the American style of using a knife and fork. The fork is held in left hand to secure food being cut with knife in the right hand. The knife is then placed across the plate and the fork is transferred to the right hand.

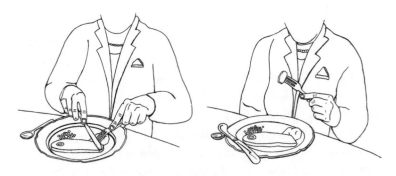

This is the European style of using a knife and fork. The fork is held in the left hand to secure food being cut with knife in the right hand. The knife is placed across plate, but the fork continues to be held in the left hand.

AMERICAN AND EUROPEAN STYLES OF CUTTING

The American custom of "zigzag" eating which involves changing the fork from left to right hand after cutting is perfectly correct, but I feel that it is unnecessarily complicated. Therefore it does not have as pleasing an appearance as the simpler European method of leaving the fork in your left hand after you have cut your food. You eat from the fork while it is still in the left hand, tines down, rather than turning it over and switching it to your right hand.

PUSHERS

When it is difficult to get such food as peas onto your fork, you may push it onto the tines instead of chasing it around the plate in a futile attempt to capture it. There is no better pusher than a piece of bread crust. Lacking this, the knife is also correct when used properly. It is held in the left hand in the same position as when cutting with the right hand, and the tip of the blade helps to guide and push the food onto the fork. It is a natural motion and in no way incorrect.

When food is difficult to get onto the fork, the knife may be used to push them onto the tines.

Your Posture

Ideal posture at the table is to sit straight, but not stiffly, leaning slightly against the back of the chair. Your hands, when you are not actually eating, may lie in your lap, which will automatically prevent you from fussing with implements, playing with bread crumbs, drawing on the tablecloth, and so forth. However, if you can't resist the temptation to fidget, you may rest your hands and wrists—but *not* your entire forearm—on the edge of the table, which may seem more comfortable and less stiff. Hands should also be kept away from the face, from nervous scratching, and from twisting or touching the hair.

For all we hear about elbows *off* the table, there are some situations when elbows are not only permitted on the table but are actually necessary. This is true in restaurants where to make oneself heard above music or conversation, one must lean far forward. A woman is far more graceful leaning forward supported by her elbows than doubled forward over her hands in her lap as though she were in pain. Elbows may also be rested on the table between courses. At home, when there is no reason for leaning across the table, there is no reason for elbows. At a formal dinner, elbows may be on the table because again one has to lean forward in order to talk to a companion at a distance across the table. But even in these special situations elbows are *never* on the table *when one is eating*.

Elbows, when not at your side or resting on the table, should *never* become wings. When cutting and eating, keep your elbows as close to your body as possible. When they are parallel to the table they not only look awkward but also are a hazard to those on either side of you.

Slouching or slumping at the table is most unattractive too. Tipping one's chair—a most unfortunate habit—is unforgivable. It not only looks dreadfully sloppy, but is fatal to the back legs of the chair.

Napkin Notes

Ordinarily, as soon as you are seated you put your napkin on your lap. At a formal dinner, however, you wait for your hostess to put hers on her lap first. It does not matter how you do it, as long as you do not give it a violent shake to open it up. You take it from the table, place it on your lap and unfold it as much as necessary with both hands.

A man should never tuck his napkin into his collar, his belt or between the buttons of his shirt.

When using the napkin, avoid wiping your mouth as if with a washcloth. Blotting or patting the lips is much more attractive.

When the meal is finished, or if you leave the table during the meal, put the napkin on the left side of your place, or if the plates have been removed, in the center. It should not be refolded, nor should it be crumpled up; rather it is laid on the table in loose folds so that it does not spread itself out. At a dinner party the hostess lays her napkin on the table as a signal that the meal is over, and the guests then lay their napkins on the table—not before.

If a family uses napkin rings, the napkins are refolded and placed in the rings and reused once or twice.

When to Start Eating

At a small table of two, four or even six people, when the delay will not be sufficient to cause the food to become cold or the soufflée to fall, it is certainly polite to wait to start eating until all have been served. In this case the hostess should pick up her implement first, and the others follow suit.

If the group is larger, however, it is *not* necessary to wait until all have been served. The hostess, if she is at all aware of her guests' comfort, will say, as soon as the first two or three guests have their food, "Please start—your dinner will get cold if you wait," and the guests take her at her word and start immediately. If the hostess says nothing, and you realize that her attention has been devoted to serving or supervising, or that she has simply forgotten to say anything, it is not incorrect to pick up your spoon or fork after five or six people have been served. The others will soon follow your lead.

At a restaurant, it is inexcusable for the waiter to bring plates for only a few people only to disappear leaving the others at the table without their food. All entrées should be brought at the same time. If they are not, those who have not yet been served should be sure to insist that those who have been served begin so that their meals do not get cold. If the entrée is cold—chef's salads, for example—then those who have been served may certainly wait for the rest of the order to arrive.

Don't Drink from the Fingerbowl!

Finger bowls are seen most often at formal dinners or when food is served that is eaten with the hands, such as lobster or crab legs. To the uninitiated, they may appear to be an unexpected course, and since they are sometimes presented with the dessert flatware on the under plate, it would be natural to pick up the spoon and begin eating from them. As with anything else to which you are unaccustomed, stop, look and listen before acting. You would not be the first person to ever drink or eat from the finger bowl, but knowing this may not make it any less embarrassing for you.

Finger bowls are usually small glass bowls filled half to three-quarters with cold water. They are used for freshening your fingers after a meal or after eating a "hands on" food such as snails, corn on the cob or hard-shelled seafood. They are placed at the upper left side of each diner's place at the end of an informal dinner, or on the dessert plate at a formal dinner.

Dip your fingers, one hand at a time, into the water and then dry your fingers on your napkin. If a finger bowl is brought directly before dessert, it is often placed on a doily on the dessert plate. To remove it, lift it with the doily underneath, and move it to the upper left of your place setting.

A slice of lemon is never used in a finger bowl at a formal dinner, but flowers may be floated in it. Lemon may be floated in a finger bowl used after a lobster dinner.

In some restaurants, moist, steamed hand towels are brought

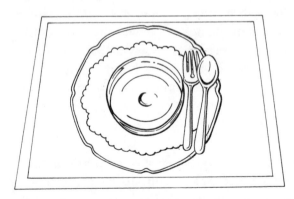

When a finger bowl is brought to the table before dessert, it is placed on the dessert plate, on top of a doily, with the dessert fork and spoon placed at the edge of the plate.

After using the finger bowl and drying ones fingers on a napkin, the guest lifts the doily and the finger bowl to the upper left of his place setting and moves the fork and spoon to the left and right side of the plate.

to the table at the conclusion of the meal. They are held in tongs and presented to the diner. Take the towel and use it to wipe your hands and if necessary around your mouth. Diligent waiters will hover and take the towel from you the minute you are finished with it. If your waiter disappears, just put the towel at the side of your place on the table. It will make the tablecloth a little wet, but you cannot be expected to sit and hold the towel, by now cool, until your waiter returns.

SERVING YOURSELF AND BEING SERVED

When helping yourself to any food, the most important thing is to pay attention to what you are doing and not handle a serving fork or spoon in such a way as to cause food to spill. When being served, the same attention is required. In neither case should you heap your plate with food. Take modest portions of those things you like, and decline, politely, those things you do not care for at all.

Passing Food Around the Table

At a dinner table where the host is filling plates and passing them around the table, they are started counterclockwise. Each diner on the right side of the table takes the plate from the person on his left and passes it to the person on his right. If there is a female guest on the host's right she keeps the first plate, but the second is passed on to the person at the end of the table. The third goes to the person farthest down on the right side, the next to the person on his left, etc. When all the people on the host's right are served, the plates are sent down the left side and the host serves himself last. If the hostess serving, the same order is followed from her end.

If the host or hostess serves the main entrée and other dishes are passed so each diner can help him- or herself, these dishes are passed counterclockwise as well. If they are all placed in front of the host, he would pick up each dish and pass it to the person on his right, one at a time. When serving dishes are placed randomly on the table, the person seated in front of each dish picks it up, helps himself and passes the dish to his right. When there is little room on the table or a serving bowl or platter is awkward, it is courteous, after helping oneself, to offer to hold the bowl for the person to one's right and for each person to then extend this courtesy around the table.

It is extremely thoughtless to help oneself and then put the dish down without making sure it has gone all the way around the table once. It is also thoughtless not to "start" a dish around the table when that dish is nearest to you. Even if you do not care for whatever it is, it is your responsibility to make sure it is passed.

When dishes are presented for guests to help themselves, the server stands to the left and the guest, using the spoon to lift a portion and the fork to balance it, transfers it to her plate.

When There is Serving Staff

Servers present a platter or bowl to the guest's left, either offering to serve a portion to the guest or holding the platter or dish in such a way that the guest may help herself. In the latter case, each dish is supplied with whatever utensils are needed for serving it. A serving spoon and a large fork are put on most dishes, or the spoon alone is used if the dish is not hard to manage when helping oneself. With the spoon held underneath in the left hand, the fork is held in the right hand with the prongs turned down to hold and balance the portion when both utensils are used.

Refusing a Dish

If you are served a food you are allergic to, or especially dislike, and if you are among friends, you may refuse with a polite "No, thank you." Otherwise it is good manners to take at least a little of every dish that is offered to you, which can be spread out on your plate so that it is barely noticeable that you have not eaten much. The old rule that one must not leave anything on his plate no longer applies, but it would be wasteful to take a large portion and leave it untouched. You need not give your reason for refusing a dish, but if it is because of an allergy, diet, or other physical cause, you may avoid hurting your hostess's feelings if you quietly tell her your problem, always without drawing the attention of the entire table.

When declining a dish offered by a waiter, you say, "No, thank you," quietly. At a buffet dinner, where there are a number of dishes offered, you need only help yourself to those that appeal to you. When there are servers behind the buffet line, hold your plate forward for those items you would like. Simply smile and say "No, thank you" when offered items you don't want.

How Much to Take, and How to Take It

The portions you take should be reasonable. This means that you should not pile your plate full of food, nor should you take a tiny spoonful.

When a platter of thinly sliced meat is offered or passed, take two pieces. When the meat is thickly sliced, take one. If the meat is tiny lamb chops or small chicken portions, take two, but if the chops or the chicken pieces are large, take only one. Take one generous spoonful of rice or potatoes, an equivalent amount of pasta that is a side dish to a main entrée, and a spoonful of vegetables. If the vegetable is asparagus, take five or six stalks. If it is a grilled tomato half, take one.

If gravy is provided and you wish to have some, it should be put on your meat, potatoes or rice, not next to them. If there is a condiment, such as cranberry jelly, it is placed at the side of whatever it accompanies, not on top of it. Other condiments, such as olives and pickles, are put on one's bread-and-butter plate, if there is one, or on the edge of the plate from which one is eating.

Anything served on a piece of toast should be lifted from the platter on the toast. Squab or quail might be lifted, leaving the toast on the plate, but foods such as mushrooms, sweetbreads or asparagus must remain on the toast. Otherwise, it would be difficult to serve them, and a soggy, unattractive piece of toast would be left on the platter. The toast with its topping is lifted on the spoon and held in place with the fork. If you don't want to eat the toast, simply put it to one side of your plate. If a fork and spoon are presented with the food, the spoon is used to scoop a portion and the fork is placed on top to balance it on its way to the plate.

MANAGING YOUR MANNERS

One of the greatest tests to a gracious diner is to be presented with any one of a series of eating difficulties that can challenge the manners of the masters. Whether an insect is spotted in your soup or you find yourself with a green vegetable wedged between your two front teeth, all your aplomb is called upon to deal with the dilemma. Stay calm. There is a way to handle every situation.

Food That is Too Hot or Spoiled

If a bite of food is too hot, quickly take a swallow of water. Only if there is no cold beverage at all, and your mouth is scalding, should you spit it out. And then it should be spit onto your fork or into your fingers, and quickly put on the edge of the plate. The same is true of spoiled food. Should you put a "bad" oyster or clam, for example, into your mouth, don't swallow it, but remove it as quickly and unobtrusively as you can. Never spit anything into your napkin.

Choking

If a sip of water does not help stop your choking but you think you can dislodge the offending bit of food with a good cough, cover your mouth with your napkin and do it. Remove the fish bone or abrasive morsel from your mouth with your fingers and put it on the edge of your plate. If you need a more prolonged bout of coughing, excuse yourself and leave the table.

In the event that you are really choking, do not hesitate to get someone to help you. When a person is truly choking, he is unable to speak, cough or make any sound whatsoever. Do whatever is necessary to attract attention to yourself if you find yourself in this position. The seriousness of your condition will quickly be recognized, and it is no time to worry about manners. Keeping calm and acting quickly might well save your life.

Coughing, Sneezing and Blowing Your Nose

It is not necessary to leave the table to perform any of these functions, unless the bout turns out to be prolonged. In that case you should excuse yourself until the seizure has passed. When you feel a sneeze or a cough coming on, cover your mouth and nose with your handkerchief, or if you do not have one, or have time to get it out, your napkin. In an emergency your hand will do better than nothing at all. Never use your napkin to blow your nose. If you are caught short without a handkerchief or a tissue, excuse yourself and head for the nearest bathroom.

Stones, Bugs, Hairs and Other Disgusting Things

When you get something that doesn't belong there into your mouth, there is no remedy but to remove it. This you do as inconspicuously as possible—spitting it quietly into your fingers. Occasionally, however, you notice the alien matter before you eat it—a hair in the butter, a worm on the lettuce, or a fly in the soup. If it is not upsetting to you, remove the object without calling attention to it and go on eating. If it is such that it upsets your stomach leave the dish untouched rather than embarrass your hostess, in a private home. At a restaurant you may—and should—point out the object to your waiter and ask for a replacement.

Food Stuck in a Tooth

Neither your fingers nor a toothpick should be wielded at the table to remove food stuck in your teeth. If you feel something wedged between your teeth or caught in your denture and it is bothering you, excuse yourself and go to the nearest bathroom to dislodge it.

If you notice a distracting bit of food stuck right in the front of a co-diner's teeth and believe she isn't aware that it is there, it is kinder to tell her, "Mary, you seem to have a little spinach caught between your teeth," than to let her go on smiling and talking only to be completely embarrassed when she discovers it later.

Spills

If you should spill a solid food on the table, pick up as much as you can neatly with a clean spoon or the blade of your knife. If it has caused a stain, dab a little water from your glass on it with a corner of your napkin. Apologize to your hostess who, one hopes, will be gracious enough not to carry on about the accident.

If you spill wine or water, get a cloth or sponge and mop up the liquid right away, helping your hostess as much as you can. In a restaurant, attract the attention of the waiter who will bring a cloth to cover the spot.

Spoons and Swizzle Sticks

When you are served a beverage with a spoon or swizzle stick (stirrer) in it, you must remove it from the glass before drinking. *Never* drink with anything, whether a paper umbrella or a teaspoon, still in the cup or glass in which it is served. At a cocktail party, you must hold the stirrer in your hand until you find a waste receptacle. At a restaurant, when there is no plate on which to put a spoon or stirrer, you should let it drip as dry as possible and place it on the table or in an ashtray if no one at the table smokes. At someone's home, you would put a spoon on the saucer, on a plate, or on a paper napkin, never on the tablecloth or on a cloth napkin. It is also acceptable, if there is absolutely nowhere to dispose of a spoon, to ask, "Where should I put this spoon?" or, if in the home of a good friend or relative, to excuse yourself for a moment and carry it to the kitchen.

DINING DO'S AND DON'T'S

Being at ease at any mealtime table means being able to thoroughly enjoy the company and the cuisine. Focusing all of your attention on doing the right thing at the right time can spoil the meal for you. A review of the following "do's" and "don't's" will help make you comfortable about the process of gracious dining.

Do remember to say "please" and "thank you" frequently. Say, "John, would you please pass the potatoes," not "Pass the potatoes." When you receive the potatoes, say, "Thank you."

Do taste before seasoning. Anyone who has worked hard to prepare a meal has to be appalled to see you drowning it in ketchup or covering it in salt before you even taste it.

Don't encircle your plate with one arm while eating with the other hand.

Don't push back your plate when finished. It remains exactly where it is until the person serving you removes it. If you wait on yourself, get up and carry it to the kitchen.

Don't lean back and announce, "I'm through," or "I'm stuffed." When you put your utensils down it shows that you have finished.

Don't *ever* put liquid into your mouth if it is already filled with food. You might have a little toast in your mouth when you drink your coffee, but it should be so little as to be undetectable by others.

Don't wipe off the tableware in a restaurant. If you do happen to find a dirty piece of silver at your place, call your waiter or waitress, show him the utensil and ask for a clean one.

Do cut your food one or two pieces at a time. Only small children may have their entire plate of food cut for them at once so that they can eat it. Cut one piece, eat it, then cut another.

Don't, if you are a woman, wear an excessive amount of lipstick to the table, out of consideration for your hostess's napkin, and also because it is very unattractive on the rim of a glass or on the silver.

Don't crook your little finger when picking up your cup. It's an affected mannerism.

Don't *ever* leave your spoon in your cup. Not only does it look unattractive, it can be dangerous.

Do eat quietly. Do not slurp, smack your lips, crunch or make other noises as you chew or swallow.

Don't leave food on your spoon or fork to be waved about during conversation. In fact, don't ever wave your utensils in the air.

Do take a manageable mouthful of what you are eating.

Do chew your food sufficiently, putting your fork down between bites. Unless you are about to catch a train, there should be no rush.

Do wipe your fingers and your mouth frequently with your napkin. Use a corner of the napkin and blot at your mouth; don't wad up the napkin and scrub your face with it.

5

Restaurant Etiquette:

Menus, Manners and Maitre d's

Restaurants are designed around the serving of meals, no matter what other entertainments they provide. Because of this, restaurant table manners begin the moment that you invite a guest to join you, the second that you make your reservation or the minute that you step in the door.

Restaurant dining is now a common rather than a special event for many people. Eating in fast-food restaurants seldom requires more than everyday good manners, while dining in more formal restaurants requires some additional knowledge, simply because it involves more dining room staff and more courses. Young children should be taught to speak quietly, and to use their best manners so that this experience is as pleasurable for other restaurant patrons as it is for your family.

There are many more special ways food in a restaurant is presented, prepared and served and they are there for you to enjoy. Do not be hesitant to order something new, or to ask how to handle it, for you will deprive yourself of experiences that add fun and interest to eating out. Maitre d's, waiters, waitresses, chefs and all other restaurant personnel are there to serve, to provide an enjoyable dining experience to entice you to return. Show your appreciation, in addition to thank-yous, through your interest and obvious enjoyment. It is always correct to thank the person who refills your water glass—there is no need to pretend he is invisible. It is always thoughtful to thank a waitress for her good service, or for bringing you a replacement fork when you have dropped yours. To be haughty or to ignore the waitstaff is neither gracious nor kind. While they are simply doing their job, they appreciate being complimented and thanked. After all, don't you feel good when your employer commends you for something you have done, or your child tells you how delicious the dinner you prepared was?

Above all else, you should enjoy any restaurant experience, whether it is a hamburger on the run at a fast-food restaurant or a seven-course dinner at an internationally acclaimed one. Knowing how to conduct yourself adds immeasurably to your comfort, allowing you to focus on the food, service, ambience, and not worry whether or not you are doing the right thing in the right way.

RESERVATIONS

Reservations are made in one name only. When calling for a reservation, advise the restaurant how many will be in your party and what time you expect to arrive. If you have any questions about the dress code of the restaurant, or whether it accepts your credit card, this is the time to ask. In addition, mention any special seating preferences you may have; by the window, or in a booth, and whether you wish to be seated in the smoking or nonsmoking section.

If your arrival is going to be delayed by more than ten minutes, you must call and change your reservation. This is a courtesy to the restaurant, the smooth operation of which is contingent upon the prompt arrival of its guests. It is also prudent to do this, for if you are late, your reserved table will likely be given away and you may be left to wait a considerable time for another.

USING A CHECKROOM

Where coat checkrooms exist, men are always expected to check their coats and any accessories. Women generally check their coats as well, although they may keep them if they tend to get chilled easily. Some checkrooms will not accept fur coats because they don't want to be responsible for them. In this case, a woman would wear her coat until she is seated and then throw the shoulders of the coat back over her chair. A man never wears a hat indoors. A woman may keep her hat on in a restaurant. It is best to check all parcels, umbrellas, etc., since there is nowhere to put them conveniently at the table. A woman keeps her handbag in her lap or places it on the floor at her feet, never on the table.

Personal objects do not belong on a restaurant table. Not eyeglasses, not cigarette packs, lighters, or pens or notebooks or presents for a host or hostess. If you have taken a gift of some sort, present it on your way out with your thanks for a lovely evening.

If a birthday party is being held in a restaurant and you are carrying a gift, it should be checked and given as you leave, unless the party is in a private room. In this case, there would likely be a table for gifts. If in doubt, ask the maitre d' if there is room for the gift or if you should check it.

When your lunch or dinner is a "working" meal, you may have papers to review. These need not be checked, since you will need them, but they should not be put on the table, either. Carry them to your place and put them under your chair, or on an empty chair if there is one, until you need them. Never pile packages, papers or anything else next to your chair where they will be in the way.

WAITING FOR OTHERS

When members of a group arrive separately at a restaurant, the first arrival should wait for the second rather than go in and sit alone, unless the first arrival sees that the restaurant is filling up and there may shortly be no tables left. When two arrive together they should ask to be seated, explaining to the head-waiter that others are joining them and asking him to see that they are promptly directed to the table. This avoids overcrowd-ing the entry and sometimes is the only way of holding a reser-vation. Some restaurants, however, will not seat a group until all members are present.

When a woman is meeting a man at a restaurant and arrives first, she may do one of several things. If she knows he has made a reservation but does not see him, she may say to the headwaiter, "I believe Mr. McCullough made a reservation for us. Would you please show me to the table and tell him I'm here when he arrives." If no reservation has been made, however, it is better for her to wait in the entry for him rather than assume the responsi-bility of choosing the table—although again she may sit down if she sees that there are few tables left. Finally, if it is a nice day, she may prefer to walk down the street, window-shopping for a few moments, and return when she is sure he has arrived. This, how-ever, is really a question of tactics rather than of etiquette.

Ideally a man waits for a woman in the entry, after first mak-ing sure that she has not been seated already. However, many city restaurants have tiny halls or entryways, and if all the peo-ple waiting for others stood there, no one could possibly get through. So if the area is crowded, or if there is danger of losing his reservation, a man may ask to be seated—especially if his companion, either male or female, is late. He should keep his eye on the door, ready to wave and rise as the other approaches, and he should tell the headwaiter whether he is expecting a woman or a man, and to please be sure that his guest is brought in at once. The person who is waiting at the table, or at a bar in the entry, may order a cocktail before the other arrives, and may even order for his companion if he knows what he or she wants, and that he or she will arrive very shortly.

WAITING AT THE BAR

Sometimes, a host elects to wait for his guest at the bar, or a party waiting for a table is told it will be another fifteen minutes until their table is ready and they prefer to go into the bar to have a drink while they wait.

If you have not finished your drink when your table is ready, what you do with your glass depends on the type of restaurant it is. In restaurants where superb service is part of the menu, the waiter will carry your glass from the bar to your table when you are being seated. If this is not the case, you may carry your own glass, if you like, or, if you have only a swallow left, finish your drink first and then proceed to your table.

Again depending on the restaurant, your bar bill is handled in different ways. In some restaurants it is expected that you pay your bar bill either when your drink is served, or before leaving the bar, leaving a tip for the bartender at the same time. In others, the bartender may offer to carry your bar bill over to your dinner bill. If this is the case, you still should leave a cash tip for the bartender before leaving the bar, for the service he has provided while you were there.

BEING SEATED

When dining alone or when hosting another or a group, one announces oneself to the restaurant host or hostess: "Good evening. I made a reservation for Demenocal, a party of four." Or, if you have no reservation, you state how many are in your party. If it is a restaurant with smoking and non-smoking sections, you should, at this time, indicate your preference.

In a group, one person, even though she or he is not paying for everyone else's meal, should serve as spokesperson and handle these arrangements.

When the table is ready the dining room host or maitre d' will lead the way. When a man and a woman are dining together, she walks directly behind the maitre d'. The man she is with follows. In a mixed group, all the women precede all the men.

When one person is hosting a group, he or she should go first to arrange seating. This precludes leaving all the guests standing and waiting for their host to bring up the rear. If guests somehow precede the host or hostess and seat themselves spontaneously around the table, it is better to leave them where they are seated than to insist that they get up and rearrange themselves according to your seating plan.

The headwaiter generally pulls out one chair to seat the woman if a couple is dining together.

If you don't like the table that has been offered you, you may always say, "We would prefer a table with a banquette (built-in seating) if there is one free," or "Could we be seated a little farther from the door, please?" If this isn't possible, you may say, "All right then, this will be fine," or, if you are really displeased, "Thanks, but I think we'll try another restaurant that isn't so crowded" or, "Thanks, but we'll wait at the bar until the table we want is available."

Where there is no waiter at hand to seat people, the man seats his female guests. If he is with two women, he helps first one and then the other. He should always seat a guest before his wife, who by that time should have seated herself.

When two couples dine, the host and hostess generally sit opposite one another. If neither couple is giving the party, the two women usually sit opposite one another. In larger groups, a guest of honor is seated to the host's or hostess's right with men and women alternating around the table. Ordinarily, men do not sit next to their wives.

When two men and a woman dine together, she is seated between them. One man would be seated between two women.

At a table with a banquette, a couple is usually seated side-by-side facing the room. Otherwise, women are seated on the banquette and men on chairs opposite them.

In a restaurant with booths, women slide in first and sit against the wall, facing one another. Men sit next to them on the outside.

HOSTING A RESTAURANT MEAL

The first thing a host must consider is the choice of restaurant. Do her guests like exotic food or good plain cooking? If guests are from out of town do they have the proper clothes with them for an elaborate restaurant? Do they wish to visit a "famous" place or would they prefer a charming inn? If a man is taking a woman to dinner would she like a small, intimate spot, or would she prefer a larger restaurant with a band and a dance floor?

When entertaining for business, with business to be discussed during the meal, the host should select a restaurant that is quiet enough to permit serious discussion, or one where there are quiet corners so that constant interruptions and noise from neighboring tables do not interfere.

The Invitation

An invitation to a restaurant meal should name the restaurant so that guests know how to dress and what to expect. When the restaurant is part of a club, or has a particular dress code, the good host will say so. It is thoughtful to say, "On Friday nights, jackets and ties are required," or "If the weather is good, we'll eat on the terrace, so be sure to bring a sweater in case the evening is cool," etc. When the restaurant is very casual, say so, or your guests may overdress and feel uncomfortable. Communicate precisely what your invitation includes, from style of dress to time. "We have an eight o'clock reservation; why don't you and Jim come by the house about seven for a drink before we leave for the restaurant." Or, "We'll meet you at the restaurant and hope you and Fran can come back to the house with us afterward for a nightcap."

If you have to cancel an invitation, do so yourself; do not have a secretary or someone else break the date. Give your reason and reschedule immediately. If the date has to be cancelled again, which can happen with hectic business schedules, immediately reschedule once again, and send a note of apology for the inconvenience you have caused. Otherwise, your guest may feel that you really don't want to see him.

In issuing an invitation, particularly a business-lunch invitation, it is courteous to select a restaurant near your guest's office. It is also courteous to make sure that your guest indeed loves Mexican food or enjoys Indian cuisine before selecting an international restaurant. Just say, "Would you like to try the new sushi restaurant near your office, or would you be more in the mood for a Cajun menu, or the English pub around the corner?" It would be most unfortunate to assume that because you love sushi, for example, your guest does too. If your guest is a new acquaintance and you are not sure what her dietary restrictions may be, it is a good idea to select a restaurant that has a varied menu. It would not do to take a vegetarian to a steakhouse unless you know the steakhouse has entrée salads, fruit plates or other nonmeat selections.

When you issue a specific invitation: "I'm calling to invite you to lunch next Thursday or Friday, whichever is better for your schedule," you are the host, and you pay the bill. This is entirely different than agreeing to meet a friend for lunch where it might be assumed that you would split the bill.

If you are a stranger to the town yet are the host for the meal, there is nothing wrong with saying, "I would like to take you to dinner, but haven't a clue as to what would be a nice restaurant. Tell me the name of your favorite place and I'll call and make a reservation for us."

Arrive Early

When your plans are to meet at the restaurant, remember that it is awkward for your guest to arrive before you since he or she won't know what arrangements you've made. Try to be at the restaurant at least five minutes early so that you can confirm your reservation and be in the foyer or at the table to welcome your guest.

If your guest is late and you are seated, you may order a drink, if you wish, but you should leave your napkin on the table and certainly should not begin eating breadsticks or crackers or anything else until he or she arrives. If you decide to wait at the table, leave the best seat for your guest. This seat would be a banquette seat, the seat with the best view, and/or the seat that is not in the direct path to the kitchen. Even when you are seated at the same time, it is up to you to ensure that the best seat is given to your guest.

When the guest arrives, a man would rise to greet him or her. A woman remains seated unless her guest is a much older woman, but would shake hands with her guest when he or she reaches the table. If you have more than one guest, plan ahead of time where you would like each to sit and say, when they arrive, "Jeannie, why don't you sit here—Terence, you sit here across from Jeannie."

The host's duties continue throughout the meal. If a host sees that her guest is not eating, she should enquire once only, "Is everything all right?" If it is not, the guest should say so—it may be that his steak is too rare, or his meal is not what he ordered. In this case, the host should take care of the error right away. If the problem is simply that the guest discovers that he really doesn't like what was ordered he probably will prefer to say nothing unless the meal is actually spoiled or tainted.

Ordering Cocktails

A guest usually takes his or her lead from the host, but when the waiter asks, "May I get you something from the bar?" and the host says, "What would you like, John?" John has an awkward moment, not knowing if his host is going to order a cocktail or a glass of iced tea. And most guests feel uncomfortable ordering a Scotch and water, for example, only to have their host ask for a glass of mineral water. It is thoughtful for the host to reply to the waiter's request immediately, so his or her guest knows what to do. If not ordering a cocktail, the host should say, "I don't think I'll have a cocktail, but please do—I'll have some sparkling water while you're having your gin and tonic." If ordering a cocktail, the host should immediately say, "I'll have a glass of white wine—what would you like, George?" George then feels comfortable ordering a cocktail, if he wishes.

Hosts should not urge guests to order cocktails if they have refused, but no guest should feel uncomfortable because he or she would like a drink when the host does not. No host should urge his guest to order a cocktail or a soft drink and then order nothing himself. If your guest orders something, even a glass of iced tea, you should follow suit.

If there are guests among a group who say no to liquor, the host should suggest that they have a soft drink while the others are having cocktails. It is impolite to order more than one or two cocktails when others are left with nothing in front of them and only the hope of a meal to sustain them.

Ordering the Meal

If the host has ordered the dinner ahead of time, he or she must try to check the dishes as they are served to make sure that everything is as requested. If there are any omissions she should quietly call them to the attention of the waiter and make sure that the missing items are supplied.

If a guest wishes a separate menu from what the host has pre-ordered, for dietary reasons only (health-related or because of a specific diet, such as a vegetarian would follow), she should ask her host: "Would it be all right if I just ordered a fruit plate?" She should do this as soon as possible, since otherwise the host will have to bear the cost of the preordered lamb chops or crab claws in addition to the special order. If this is necessary, the guest should quietly explain why she is unable to eat what everyone else is eating. Naturally, no guest would do this in someone's home but would rather just eat what she could from what was served.

If dinner has not been ordered beforehand, it can be the host's duty to take the guests' orders and give them to the waiter. If the party is large, the host makes sure that the waiter gets the order correctly from each person. Again, if there are mistakes, the host must tactfully and politely see that they are corrected, without embarrassing the guests. There is nothing wrong with each guest giving his or her own order to the waiter. Often, the waiter will say, "Are you ready to order?" to the host and, if the answer is affirmative, he circles the table and takes an order from each diner directly. If there is a guest of honor, the host or hostess should look at her and say, "Why don't you start, Sue," and the waiter moves around next to her chair. If there is no guest of honor any one of the women who is ready orders first. Individual ordering is certainly less confusing, and there will be fewer mistakes made, especially if the group is large.

When a couple is dining together and the waiter looks directly at a woman and asks, "What kind of dressing would you like on your salad?" it is absurd and insulting if she turns away from the waiter and relays her response through her escort. Many waiters ask the woman for her order first in an effort to be polite, and there is no reason why she should not answer directly.

If a guest needs something, however, he should indicate his

request through his host and not summon the waiter himself.

A good host will help his or her guests with their selections. If the restaurant is famous for certain menu items, let your guests know. If the sky is the limit, the host should mention a few items in the most expensive price range: "The lobster here is wonderful, and their steak au poivre is the best I've ever had." This gives a guideline to guests that they shouldn't look for the bargain item to order.

At the same time, the host should indicate that guests are to order courses, not just an entrée. "The crab cakes are excellent, and both the Caesar's salad and the mixed green salad are superb."

If the host has never eaten in the restaurant, he still should help the guests know how to order. "I think I might begin with the New England clam chowder followed by the mixed green salad, although I'm really tempted by the shrimp scampi appetizer and the radicchio salad. . . " There should be no hesitation about asking the waiter to recommend one of the specialties of the restaurant, either, again indicating the number of courses guests should consider ordering.

When a host does not do this, the guest should ask for a table d'hôte dinner if one is offered, or choose only an entrée and a salad if it is not. The host may always add more, with the guest's approval, but no guest wants to blithely order an appetizer and then be the only one at the table having one. When uncertain and with no lead from a host, a guest should order neither the most expensive nor the least expensive item on the menu, but select one from the middle range.

Usually a waiter either presents a dessert menu or lists those items available for dessert. The host should urge his guests to order dessert. If only one or two do, the host should also order a dessert so they don't feel uncomfortable for having done so. A guest may, of course, order only coffee or tea, even when urged to order a dessert to accompany it.

Ordering Wine

For those who prefer a glass of wine to a cocktail that is naturally ordered before the meal with the cocktail order. Bottles of wine should be ordered after the choices for the meal have been made, from the wine steward if there is one, or from the waiter if there is not. The host, or whoever may be best qualified, should choose a wine that goes well with the greatest number of choices of food. For instance, if more people have ordered chicken or fish, choose a white wine, but if more are having a steak dinner, pick a red. Or a bottle of each may be ordered. There are many people who enjoy a vin rosé, or pink wine, and it is often a happy compromise, as it goes well with many menu items. Most restaurants also offer wine by the glass, and that is an ideal solution when two people dining together want different wines or they do not want as much as a bottle contains.

If you have a definite preference for red or white wine it is not incorrect to order either with any food. The choices stated above are simply those which, for the majority, result in the most pleasing combination of flavors.

You may choose imported wines if you wish, but there are many excellent domestic wines available. One should not feel it necessary to spend a great deal to enjoy a good wine with dinner. If you do not recognize the names on the wine list, by all means ask the wine steward's or headwaiter's advice, giving him an idea of the type you prefer and whether domestic or imported.

When you are a guest and nothing is said by your host about ordering wine, it is impolite to broach the subject yourself.

The wine, when brought to the table, is always offered to the host. In some restaurants the wine steward offers the opened cork to the host. The host might examine the cork to make sure it does not have a moldy smell, which would be a sign that the wine was not stored properly. The wine steward then pours a small amount into the host's glass. He may either sniff the aroma, or take a small sip, or both. Any wine that tastes sour or vinegary or moldy is probably spoiled. If the host isn't sure, he should ask the opinion of the wine steward or the waiter. If there is definitely something wrong with the wine, the bottle should be removed and another brought. If it seems fine, the host nods his approval, or says, "Fine," and the guest's glasses are filled, with the host's glass filled last.

READING MENUS

Table d'hôte means a set price for a complete meal, regardless of how many courses are included. "Club" breakfasts and lunches, "blue-plate" dinners, or any meals at fixed prices *(prix fixé)* are table d'hôte.

À la carte means that you order from a list of dishes and you pay the price listed beside each dish for everything from salad to coffee.

Usually it is very easy to know which is which, because a price follows each item on an à la carte menu. No prices are listed on some table d'hôte bills of fare except at the top where the price for the complete dinner may be printed.

Another type of table d'hôte menu is the one that has a price beside each entrée. This price includes the choice of an appetizer or a soup, a salad, and a dessert, and choice of coffee, tea or milk. If any other items on the menu are followed by a price, there is an additional charge for them.

Very often a separate card or a box insert on the à la carte menu reads, "Special dinner $24.00," or whatever the price may be, and informs you that you can order whatever you choose on this special for twenty-four dollars, but that any item taken from the regular bill of fare will be charged as an extra.

A very few exclusive restaurants hand a guest a menu that has no prices on it. Presumably if the host has chosen the restaurant, he is prepared to pay for whatever the guest selects.

Although many guests are made very uncomfortable when this occurs, there is little to do except order what you like. However, if you suspect the host or hostess had not realized that the restaurant made a practice of doing this, you can select an item that is ordinarily lower-priced—a chicken dish instead of filet mignon, for example.

When a waiter or waitress recites a list of specials without telling you the prices, it is difficult to know the price range they are in. It is embarrassing for either guest or host to ask. I wish restaurants would recognize this and either clip a handwritten "specials" menu, which includes prices, to the main menu, or instruct the waiters to state the price after describing the special.

At a club, menus often do not include prices other than on the host's menu. Since it is to be presumed that the host has eaten at the club before, he is in a position to make recommendations and he should, just as in a public restaurant. His suggestions give the guests an idea of how they should order.

ASKING FOR RECIPES

Well-known restaurants sometimes publish cookbooks of their recipes. If you have enjoyed your meal, or a certain dish in particular, and wish to obtain its recipe ask the headwaiter or maitre d' if the restaurant publishes a cookbook. If they do, you may even find it for sale at the restaurant. If they do not, ask if the chef ever provides recipes and what the charge might be. Some restaurants offer preprinted recipes to customers, free of charge, whenever they ask. Others do not.

SPECIAL REQUESTS

For dietary or other reasons, it may be that you wish to enquire about the possibility of ordering a deviation from the way a food is offered. My niece loves breaded cutlet, but not with tomato sauce or cheese covering it. Most Italian restaurants where a plain cutlet is not on the menu are happy to agree. When each order is prepared fresh, this kind of request, which is the elimination of a topping, and so on, is no problem.

Many Chinese restaurants offer items with or without monosodium glutamate (MSG); others do not. Some luncheon restaurants offer reduced-calorie versions of other items, or variations on a theme, indicating their flexibility. There is a limit to what you may request, however. You should not request a listed basil tomato sauce without the basil, as an absurd example, because it most likely is already simmering in a pot, basil included. Nor should you even think of asking for your baked alaska to be made with no sugar, or for tarragon to be added to the au jus part of your roast beef au jus order. These kinds of requests are insulting to the chef who has worked hard to plan a combination of tastes and flavors, and they are inexcusably demanding, requiring the full attention of one chef to prepare your order to different specifications. If you want tarragon-flavored au jus, fix it yourself at home.

You may, upon seeing chopped steak on the menu, ask if a smaller patty could be prepared for a young child in your party. You also may ask for sauces and dressings to be served on the side. Filet mignon with béarnaise sauce may be served with the sauce artfully poured over the meat. There is no reason that sauce can't be put in a small side dish for you. Salads often are tossed in the kitchen with the dressing you have selected. You certainly may ask for an undressed salad, with the dressing on the side.

RESTAURANT TABLE MANNERS

Although table manners are much the same whether you are eating at home or in a restaurant, there are a few special problems that do arise when dining out. *(For the particulars of eating different foods see also Chapter Four, beginning on page 118.)*

Individual Side Dishes

Many restaurants serve vegetables and potatoes in small individual side dishes, which the waiter places strategically around your dinner plate. You may eat these vegetables directly from the small dishes, or you may put them on your dinner plate by using a serving spoon or by sliding them directly out of the small dish. You may then ask the waiter to remove the empty dishes, to avoid overcrowding the table.

Cutting Bread and Pouring Coffee

When an uncut loaf of bread is placed on the table, the host slices or breaks off two or three individual portions and offers them with the rest of the loaf in the bread basket or on the plate to the people beside him. This is then passed around the table, and each man should cut or break off a portion for himself and for the woman next to him.

If the bread is in front of another at the table, he or she should simply begin by helping himself and passing the basket counterclockwise to the person next to him.

If coffee or tea is placed on the table without first having been poured by the waiter, the person nearest the pot should offer to pour, filling his or her own cup last.

Individual-Size Paper Containers

Many accompaniments to restaurant meals are often served with paper wrappers, such as sugar packets, or in cardboard or plastic containers. The question of what to do with them when emptied comes up frequently. Sugar packets should be crumpled up tightly and either tucked under the rim of your plate or placed on the edge of the saucer or butter plate. Do not put them in the ashtray as they could catch on fire, unless there are no smokers at the table.

When jelly or marmalade is served in a paper or plastic container it should be removed with the butter knife, or dinner knife if there is no butter knife, and put on the butter plate. The top is put back in the empty container, which is left on the table beside the butter plate.

Individual plastic milk or half-and-half containers should also be left on the table next to the coffee cup.

Pouring Wine

When the wine steward does not return to pour wine after initially opening the bottle and pouring the first glass, the host or hostess may remove the bottle from the wine bucket, wiping off any water from the outside, and refill glasses, beginning with guests.

Tasting Another's Food

Occasionally diners who have ordered different dishes wish to taste some of the others. This is permissible if done unobtrusively. If Cassie wants to try Andrea's moussaka, she would hand her fork to Andrea who would pick up a bit of the moussaka and hand it back to Cassie carefully. Cassie should not reach over and spear it herself, nor should Andrea use her fork to give Cassie the taste, unless she does so before she uses it herself.

It is also permissible for one person to pass the other his plate before either starts eating, so the second could put a small portion of her dessert on the edge of the plate.

At a restaurant where food is brought to the table in serving dishes to be transferred to your plate (most Chinese restaurants, for example) it is of course permissible for guests to decide that they will share. In this case, serving spoons are used to serve oneself. Plates, if passed, are passed counterclockwise around the table.

Visiting and Table-Hopping

When a group enters a restaurant and sees people whom some know and others do not, they continue directly to their table, nodding "hello" as they pass. A public restaurant is scarcely the place for mass introductions, although there are occasions when one or two introductions are suitable.

All men at a small table rise when a woman is being introduced, as they do whenever a woman stops to talk. When the group is large only those closest to the visitor rise. Because restaurant spaces are small and a group suddenly standing around the table takes up considerable room, the woman should tell the men to please be seated after they have risen. If a woman stopping at a table is introduced to other women seated there, the latter never rise—even when they are younger than the visitor.

All the men at the table do not rise when another man stops on his way by. When someone comes up to speak to one of the diners, that man only should stand to shake hands. The visitor should then ask him please to be seated while he finishes what he has come to say. No visitor should say more than a few words of greeting, for he is interrupting the group's meal, which will get cold, and is probably blocking the path of the waiters.

When a man is seated on a banquette and someone—man or woman—stops by to say hello, he merely nods and extends his hand. He need not rise, in fact, probably cannot rise, for if he tried, he would either get leg cramps from hovering in a crouched position or he would upset the table trying to straighten up!

Telephone Calls

There is only one reason to receive telephone calls at a restaurant—to be notified of an emergency that cannot wait until you have returned to your office or home. Unfortunately, there are those who will instruct someone to call them at a specific time, or who will ask that a telephone be brought to the table, simply to look important. I recall having breakfast one morning at a hotel in Beverly Hills, California, being surrounded by men talking on the telephone, each one naming astronomical sums in loud voices. I presumed that they were doing this so that anyone listening, and it was difficult not to hear, would think them amazingly powerful and important. This is pompous when dining alone; it is exceptionally rude when dining with others who must sit silent while you talk on the phone.

In a true emergency, whether called to the telephone or on a telephone brought to you, it is polite to make the call as short as possible. If it is necessary to leave the restaurant, when you are the host, you must explain, and if your guests are in the middle of the meal, you must insist that they remain and finish without you, being sure to settle the bill before you leave. If you are a guest, you must also explain and apologize for having to depart quickly.

Doggie Bags

For many years, I resisted the temptation to approve of doggie bags on the theory that while it was all right to ask to take home a bone, literally, for the dog, it was rather degrading to take home table scraps for the family. I suddenly realized that I had quite happily done just what I had advised others not to do when I was in restaurants where the servings were more than generous and I had left more on my plate than I had eaten.

If a waiter offers to wrap the remainder of your meal for you to take home, there is absolutely no reason to refuse, unless you are going on to the theater or another entertainment where you do not wish to arrive carrying an aluminum plate or a bag full of food. If the waiter does not offer and you wish to have your leftover food, just ask him to please have it wrapped so you can take it with you. Although this is totally appropriate in most restaurants, I would not recommend asking for a doggie bag in an extremely formal restaurant.

Summoning a Waiter

There is no hard or fixed rule for the best way to summon a waiter. In fact, ways that are considered proper in some countries are downright insulting in others. For example, a waiter who is hissed, whistled or clapped at in the United States would probably run in the other direction, and yet those gestures are perfectly correct in certain other nations. The usual way in the United States is to catch the waiter's attention by making eye contact while raising your hand slightly, finger pointed up, as if to say "Attention." If your waiter refuses to look in your direction, you may call "Waiter" quietly, or if he is too far away to hear you, ask any other waiter nearby, "Please call our waiter." Do not ever wave your hand wildly in the air or sit impatiently with it extended over your head, waiting to attract your waiter's attention. "Miss" is a correct term for a waitress, as is "Waitress," but "Sir" is *not* correct for a waiter.

Dropping Things

In someone's home, you would automatically pick up a dropped item, whether a fork or a napkin, and help wipe up a spill. In a restaurant, you may pick your fork up from the floor if it falls close to you and set it to one side until you can summon your waiter to ask for a replacement. If it falls some distance away, leave it until a waiter can remove it. The same is true of any other tableware you may drop.

When you drop a forkful of meat or some other small food item, such as a pea or a lettuce leaf, leave it. This is not considered a spill in a restaurant and whoever cleans up the table after your departure will sweep or clean under the table as well as on top of the table. Only when your spill is large enough to be noticeable, or affect others' safety, as when a full water glass is knocked over, is the waiter urgently called to deal with it.

Smoking

Even in a smoking section of a restaurant, refrain from smoking until dessert is finished. Although some do smoke between courses, the very act kills taste buds, offends diners at nearby tables, and is unpleasant for those with you who are still eating. When the meal is finished and coffee has been served, you should obtain the permission of others at your table before lighting a cigarette. Do not smoke a cigar or pipe in a restaurant. Cigar and pipe smoke is simply too strong to others who are dining.

Alien Objects in Your Food

Unlike dining at someone's home where you do your best to remove and ignore something that does not belong in your food, at a restaurant you summon the waiter and ask for a replacement. Do not make a scene. There are many jokes about a patron demanding in a loud voice, "What is that fly doing in my soup, waiter?" and the waiter answering, "The backstroke, sir." While the situation is not humorous, it is not necessary for you to carry on, for surely the offending object was not put there intentionally.

If you are injured by an unexpected piece of shell, bone or something else in your food, quietly let the waiter and the restaurant manager know. They should know so they can take steps to prevent it from happening to others.

Grooming at the Table

No one, ever, should comb his or her hair at any table where food is served, regardless of whether it has been cleared or not. Never rearrange or put your hands to your hair in any place where food is served.

I prefer that no grooming of any sort take place at the table. It is not unacceptable, however, to use pressed powder or lipstick—absolutely nothing else—quickly and briefly, at the end of the meal.

Voicing Complaints and Compliments

One should complain in a restaurant when the service is bad, when a waiter is rude or careless or when the food comes in badly prepared or not as ordered. These are legitimate reasons for speaking up, and it is to the restaurant's advantage that you do speak up. Its livelihood depends on customers' approval, and if its faults are not called to the management's attention they cannot be corrected.

Never complain bitterly in front of your guests. A public humiliation is not necessary, no matter how heinous the crime. Save your criticisms of terrible service for after the departure of your guests, or call or write the next day. If it is necessary to complain in person, at that moment, then please do so privately and quietly, without attracting the attention of other diners. Complain first to the waiter (or the person who commits the error). If this person makes no effort to correct the situation, the headwaiter or whoever is in charge of the dining room should be notified. Food that is cold should be taken back to be heated; meat that is not cooked as you requested should be replaced. Rudeness and laziness should be reported, but laziness or inattention should not be confused with pure inability to serve too many people. Often a waiter or waitress, because the tables are poorly allotted, or because another waiter is absent, works as hard and as fast as possible but still cannot keep up with the requests of the patrons. Diners should recognize this and make allowances. They may complain to the manger, so that more help can be sent to their area, but they should be careful not to put the blame on the waiter, who is no happier about the situation than they are.

If, after making a legitimate complaint, you receive no satisfaction from anyone, you may reduce your tip or leave none at all, and avoid that restaurant in the future.

If the experience was so terrible as to be embarrassing, you will no doubt apologize to any guests. But, although you may feel upset about whatever was wrong with the meal or the service, it was surely beyond your control and you should not continue to apologize at length. Your guests will realize the fault was with the restaurant, not with you.

I do have to note that people seem to voice their complaints much more often—and more loudly—than they voice their appreciation. Appreciative comments, as well as appreciation shown by a generous tip, are more than welcome. The tip is expected, but the extra "Thank you," "The meal was truly outstanding," or "The service was especially good," mean a great deal to someone who is trying to do his best. They also mean a great deal to the management, whose reputation is greatly enhanced by the customer who is satisfied and doesn't hesitate to say so.

It is also very thoughtful to send your compliments to the chef, but you should not request his or her presence at the table unless the meal has been especially prepared for your group (a banquet or special dinner at a private club, for example) or is so extraordinary as to mandate thanks in person. To do this, ask your waiter to see if the chef can come out for just a minute—and that's all it should be since chefs don't have more than that to spare out of the kitchen. As host or hostess, shake his or her hand and express your appreciation, perhaps referring to a specific item.

Respecting Privacy

Whether in a fast-food restaurant or an exclusive, very expensive one, your attention is at your own table, on your companion or companions, your guests or your host. No matter how clearly you can hear the conversation at a neighboring table, you must pretend that you don't. While you may be tempted to jump in and answer a question, make a comment or recommend a menu choice, don't. If you are dining alone, you must gaze, as though deep in contemplation, at the centerpiece or the wall across the room; never stare at those at another table.

Should someone at your table direct your attention to another table, for whatever reason, you must make very sure that you do not appear to be staring or gawking at another person. This is particularly unsettling when more than one person is directing his or her attention toward another. Even though you may be exclaiming over the centerpiece, it will look as though you are talking about the person.

The only time that you intervene in the business at another table is when someone is obviously in distress and you are able to help, either by administering the Heimlich maneuver or assisting in some other way. If you can't help, don't be part of a crowd that stands in a circle and stares. If you can help, do so immediately.

At a Mealtime Business Meeting

Breakfast, lunch, tea, dinner and cocktails are all times when two or more people may meet to combine a business meeting with refreshment. This is a pleasant way to meet, but it carries with it a few additional guidelines.

- Do not write on tablecloths or other table linen to illustrate something you are explaining. This is unspeakably thoughtless. Take paper with you and use it.

- Do not cover the table with papers. This makes it extremely difficult for waiters to serve you.

- Do not leap immediately into the purpose of the meeting; allow at least ten minutes for small talk. As a host, it is your responsibility to get to the heart of the matter and begin the business discussion. As a guest, you may not be the one to initiate the business portion of your meeting. It is the host's prerogative to begin this conversation. If you are meeting at mutual suggestion and neither is host nor guest, than either one of you may get to the point fairly quickly.

PAYING THE CHECK

When everyone is finished eating, the host or spokesperson for the group catches the eye of the waiter or headwaiter and says, "May I have the check, please?" The check is brought, usually face down on a small plate or tray, and is presented to the person who requested it or who ordered the meal. He or she looks at it, checks it quickly for mistakes and returns it to the plate with the money when paying in cash. If an error has been found, the waiter is called and the error quietly pointed out. The waiter or the headwaiter makes the adjustment. In no circumstances should a scene be made. When any change due is returned the host or hostess leaves the correct amount for the tip on the tray or plate.

Many restaurants ask their customers to pay a cashier on the way out. This practice is especially common in large-city restaurants and in those that are used mostly at the lunch hour. It is a great time-saver, as very often a waiter, when he has finished serving a table, gives his attention to other customers, and those waiting for their checks or change find it difficult to attract his attention. When you read at the bottom of your check, "Please pay cashier," put the tip on the table, collect your belongings and leave, with the host following the group, who wait in the entry while he pays the bill. If he needs change in order to have the right amount for a tip, he pays the check and quickly returns to the table and leaves it there.

Credit Cards

When a credit card is used, the host reviews the check, signs it and places the signed check and his credit card on the tray. The waiter returns with a charge slip. The host adds a tip, totals the bill with the tip added in, signs the charge slip and places it back on the tray. He may, if in a hurry, detach his copy and leave at that time, or he may wait for the waiter to return and detach it for him.

Splitting the Check

The very best way to share expenses in a restaurant is to ask for separate checks at the time your order is placed. This usually is not a problem when only two or three are dining together. It is a problem when the group is larger, requiring the waiter to keep track of several order forms for one table. In this case, it is better to have one bill and have one person in the group be responsible for reviewing it and doing the math, letting each person know what he or she owes, including tip. If everyone has chosen items that cost more or less the same amount, it is best to ask each for the same amount of money. But if some have only had a soup or a salad, while others dined on steak and lobster, the one in charge should make appropriate allowances.

When one person has invited another to lunch, the one extending the invitation pays for the lunch. If you are someone's guest, please do not suddenly try to reach for the check or say, "Oh no, no, this is my treat." It is not your treat; you may reciprocate soon, at which time it will be.

When two associates or two friends agree to meet for lunch with neither having invited the other, it is assumed that they will each pay for their own meal. If one indicates that he will pay the bill, the other should say, "No, Bill, thanks so much, but I'm paying my share. This way we can get together more often." It is really very tiresome when people struggle over the bill with each insisting that he or she is treating. It is far better to settle this matter before even entering the restaurant so that you do not make a spectacle of yourselves at the table.

When you are someone's guest, it is most impolite to lean over and examine the check. While the host is checking the bill, you might be silent for a minute or two as he does his mental math, but you should resume conversation shortly thereafter, expressing your thanks after the bill has been paid and you are departing from the table. You should not offer to leave the tip or make any comment at all about the bill during the entire process.

TIPPING

Overall, I believe that a tip should be merited. Where service is bad and the personnel is deliberately rude, inattentive or careless, the amount of your tip should be reduced. If it is bad *enough* and is strictly the responsibility of the waiter, not of a slow kitchen or the fact that there is inadequate service for the number of tables to be served, no tip should be left at all, and you should bring the situation to the attention of the manager.

Service Charges

In most American restaurants, the tip is left to the customer to leave or not. In others, and in most European restaurants, a service charge is automatically added to the bill. Generally, you are not expected to give an additional tip. In Europe you may leave the small coins the waiter brings back in change but you should never add the equivalent of another dollar or two.

When a service charge is added in American restaurants and in most European restaurants, the wait staff receives a higher salary. The gratuity goes to the management as part of the income of the restaurant, and the waiter keeps any small coins left on the table. In a restaurant where no service gratuity is added to the bill, the wait staff receives a minimum salary and makes up the difference with tips. Sometimes the tips are kept in their entirety by the waiter; sometimes they are put in a common pool and shared equally by all the staff at the end of the day.

How Much Is Enough?

The average gratuity is between 15 and 20 percent of the total bill before taxes. In family-style restaurants 15 percent is still the norm; in more formal, elegant restaurants, the norm is closer to 20 percent. It is difficult to give definite rules for tipping, because amounts depend upon where you go and the service that is given you. That is, if you patronize luxurious restaurants or if you have special requirements or are difficult to please, larger tips are expected than if you choose simpler restaurants and receive less service.

When there is a wine steward, the price of the wine is not included in the total that you use as the base for determining your tip. The wine steward is tipped at least two dollars a bottle, usually not more than five, even when the wine is lavishly expensive. You would hand a wine steward's tip directly to him, not include it on the table with the waiter's tip. When your waiter takes care of your wine order, the price of the wine is included in the calculation for his tip.

Like the waiter, the dining room captain depends on tips for a living wage. Leaving him 5 percent in addition to what you leave the waiting staff is adequate. Or, if his service to you has been extraordinary, and he has worked side by side with your waiter, you may divide the total tip leaving 75 percent to the waiting staff and 25 percent to the captain. Some credit card slips used in more exclusive restaurants now have two lines for tips—one for the waiter and one for the captain. Naturally, if you have not seen the captain throughout your meal, you would not add a gratuity to this line. If paying by credit card and there is no line for a gratuity for the captain and you wish to leave him one, you would hand it to him directly, in cash.

The maitre d' is not tipped, nor would you tip a host or hostess, unless you are a regular patron of the restaurant, in which case you should tip $5 to $10 *once in a while* if he or she remembers your favorite wine, for example, or makes sure that you are seated and served carefully and promptly. Never try to bribe a maitre d' for a "good" table. Do tip him if you have worked with him in advance to plan or arrange a large dinner party or special occasion.

As a guest at a large party you would assume that gratuities for table service have been taken care of by your host. If there is a private checkroom for your party or if you have used valet parking, you might check whether he has taken care of gratuities. If so, you would not duplicate them. In most cases, guests would take care of gratuities for extra services, as discussed below.

In a fine restaurant these guidelines can be helpful:

The bartender is tipped before you leave the bar, whether you pay your bar bill before departing or it is carried over onto your dinner bill. The price of drinks is such today that a tip should be from 50 cents to $1 for one or two drinks, depending on the type of restaurant or bar.

When you have two or more drinks at a bar in a nicer restaurant, you do not pay as you order, but rather when you are ready to leave, adding the tip at that time. In other bars, it is expected that you pay for each drink as you receive it, but you may wait until you depart to leave a tip.

In a bar with table service, the waiter or waitress is the one tipped, not the bartender.

The restroom attendant is tipped $1; she is tipped $2 if she does something special for you, like providing needle and thread, helping with a spot or stain, etc. In any event, she is tipped no less than 50 cents for doing nothing more than handing you a paper towel. There is always a small plate with a few coins or a dollar bill on it in a conspicuous place to remind you, and your tip is placed there, not handed to the attendant.

The checkroom attendant is tipped $1 per coat; she is tipped $2 if you have left bags, packages, gifts, umbrellas and other miscellany in addition to your coat.

A doorman who gets a taxi for you is given from $1 to $5, depending on how hard he worked to hail it. He is not tipped just for opening the hotel or taxi door for you.

A valet parking attendant is given $3 for bringing your car to you in most cities. In less expensive areas $1 to $2 is acceptable. Valet parkers are not tipped when you arrive, only upon departure. Even when a different attendant from the one who took your car brings it back, only the latter is tipped. Usually, valet attendants pool and split their tips at the end of the evening.

Busboys are not tipped.

Musicians who stroll among tables are tipped around $2 when you make a special request and they play it for you. Otherwise, when they simply stand by your table and play, moving on afterward, you tip them $1, whether you've asked them to play for you or not. If you find them particularly annoying, or they arrive at the moment you are sharing a sensitive story, proposing to the woman or man you hope will be your future spouse, or closing a dramatic business deal, you may feel comfortable asking them to play elsewhere. Simply shake your head, with a smile, and indicate that you would like them to leave your table.

When you enjoy their serenade, it is not expected that you put down your fork and gaze at them as they perform, even though it may seem awkward to keep eating and your instinct is to give them your undivided attention. A song can take anywhere from two to five minutes, during which time your just-delivered cheese soufflé is rapidly deflating. Keep eating, but do smile and say, "Thank you" when they finish, as you hand them your tip.

A RESTAURANT PARTY

Entertaining in a restaurant or club on a larger scale than just a few friends for lunch or dinner requires advance planning to ensure that the occasion is as pleasurable as possible. These arrangements can include a special dinner party for a guest of honor, a birthday party, and a wedding reception. Usually, you would work with the restaurant manager or maitre d' to discuss menu and any other details important for your party, such as linens, decorations, the setting up of favors, place cards or menu cards and gratuities. When you wish to provide your own items, such as table linens, chocolates for the table, a bakery cake, or even guest soaps and towels in the restrooms, you should discuss these details and make sure there are no problems involved in doing this.

Usually the gratuities for this kind of party are added to the bill. The tips for the waiters are divided among them and the host is not obligated to tip an additional amount unless he wishes to for outstanding service. After a large dinner or party the host should, in addition, give the person in charge, whether headwaiter or maitre d', a separate tip of no less than $25.

If no service charge is added to the bill, the host gives the person in charge approximately 20 percent of the total and asks that he or she divide it among the waiters.

International Restaurants

One of the pleasures of our increasingly international cities and towns is the variety of restaurant experiences available to patrons. It used to be rare to be able to experience Middle Eastern cuisine unless actually in the Middle East. No longer. One of the great pleasures of restaurant dining is the opportunity to try new foods. Proprietors of international restaurants are delighted to be able to share their culinary pleasures with new "audiences," and expect to be asked to describe menu items and to help with new dining experiences.

Do not hesitate to ask, "What ingredients are used in this dish?" or "What is the best way to eat this?" when you are not sure. This surely is preferable to sitting and staring at something you have never had before, unsure as to whether you are expected to tackle it with your hands, your fork or your spoon.

It is also a good idea to ask about the quantity provided as one portion. Sometimes one appetizer is enough to be shared by two people while a main course portion is so modest as to be enough just for one. For example, in a Thai restaurant, as in a

Chinese restaurant, each person at the table might order a different dish, to be shared with everyone else.

Smorgasbord or Buffet Restaurants

The smorgasbord, an import from Sweden originally, has gained tremendous popularity in the United States. Actually it is a buffet, but a buffet of such variety and interest that it is more than worth the effort of serving yourself.

Everyone at the table, unless infirm or unable to manage walking and carrying a plate simultaneously, goes to the buffet tables to help him- or herself after initially being seated by the maitre d' or dining room host or hostess and invited to do so.

Usually, a waiter or waitress takes a beverage order at the table.

Individual tables are set as usual. The smorgasbord, which literally translated means "sandwich table," has one or more stacks of small plates to be filled with reasonable amounts of food. Since you are expected to make as many trips as you wish from your seat to the smorgasbord and back, don't overload your plate and only choose foods that go well together each time you serve yourself. Leave your used plate and silver at your table for the waiter to remove while helping yourself to your next selection. Never carry a used plate back to the smorgasbord in a restaurant. It is intended that you take your time, and you should select foods in the order you would eat them were you to be ordering from a menu—appetizer, soup, fish course, etc., through dessert. Sometimes dessert and usually coffee and tea are requested from the waiter, not set on a separate smorgasbord table.

Oriental Restaurants

Japanese and Chinese restaurants offer interesting variations in service and food. Many Japanese restaurants expect that guests will remove their shoes, don paper slippers and sit on cushions on the floor at low tables, Japanese-style. If you have very long legs, like my husband, or if you are taking older or handicapped people to such a restaurant, you would never sit in that section but would request a regular table, which is always available for those who prefer it.

Chinese restaurants have regular seating arrangements. If you find chopsticks at your place and wish to use them to eat, do so. But if you feel awkward with them or cannot manage them, do not hesitate to ask for a fork and a knife. In Chinese restaurants diners at one table often order different dishes that are placed in the center of the table so that everyone may serve him- or herself from any or all of them. This is a delightful way to experiment with various dishes—and one that may be helpful in ordering the next time you go to a similar restaurant. Do not assume, however, that your companions expect to share. It is not polite to reach out and help yourself to someone else's entrée unless you have all agreed ahead of time that you will share.

OTHER KINDS OF RESTAURANTS

Cafeterias

Unlike a smorgasbord, a cafeteria is a completely self-service restaurant. You are not even seated by restaurant personnel. Upon entering you may place your coat or belongings at a table and then go to the cafeteria line. When the restaurant is crowded and there are no empty tables, it is perfectly all right in a cafeteria to take an empty chair at a table already occupied. One should say, however, "Is this seat taken?" or "Do you mind if I sit here?" Diners who join a stranger are under no obligation to talk, but it is all right to open a casual conversation if the other person seems to be receptive. If he or she does not respond after an opening gambit don't continue with further remarks. If you are joined by a garrulous stranger who will not take the hint when you do not engage in lively patter, you may say, "I'm sorry, but I am rather preoccupied at the moment and just can't concentrate on conversation." Normally busboys are not tipped, however, when they carry the trays to the tables they may be tippped, depending on the cafeteria and the amount of food on your tray.

Lunch Counters

Orders at a lunch counter are placed with the counter attendant and served from behind the counter. When a couple goes to a lunch counter that is so crowded that there are not two seats together, it is permissible to ask a person sitting between two empty stools if he or she would mind moving down one place. Conversely, a person in this position should offer to move before being asked.

Unless there is a sign that says No Tipping, tips are expected. The minimum—for a cup of coffee only—is twenty cents or a quarter. When food is served, the tip should not be less than fifty cents, more usually around 15 percent of the bill before tax.

The bill is either paid at one's seat, or taken to the cashier at the end of the counter.

Coffee Shops and Delicatessens

Most coffee shops have both booths and tables or counters for customers. These are served by waiters or waitresses. Delicatessens often have tables for customers but no waiters. In this case, the order is placed at the counter by the customer and then picked up when ready and taken to the table, or delivered by a counter person. The customer is expected to clear the table and dispose of paper plates, plastic utensils, etc., upon leaving. No tips are expected in this instance.

Fast-Food Restaurants

Like most delicatessens, fast-food restaurant service is self-service. The customer waits in line, places his or her order, receives a tray and carries it to a table, if eating in. If taking the food out, the customer receives the food in bags or cardboard carrier trays.

One of the reasons for the relatively inexpensive food in fast-food restaurants is the low overhead for salaries. There are no busboys or waiters to clear used containers from the tables. The patrons are expected to clean up after themselves when they go. It is extremely rude not to do so, or to leave a mess behind for the next patron to reach your vacated table. You are not expected to wash or scrub your table or seat—there is maintenance personnel to do this—but you are expected to place wrappers, uneaten food and other debris on your tray and slide it off into the receptacle provided.

Just because a restaurant does not have linen tablecloths and crystal glasses does not mean that you can cast your table manners to the wind. Posture, eating habits and noise levels are just the same as though you were in a four-star restaurant. Children should not be allowed to roam, food should not be strewn about, and messes should not be made.

Do not linger, either. When you are finished with your meal, leave. Fast food does not just mean instant hamburgers or already-cooked chicken wings. It also means that patrons eat and run. Not literally, but this is not the place to dawdle, if there are others waiting for a table. If you are engrossed in a conversation, continue it outside, or during a walk around the block, or in the car, or whatever so that someone else who is standing there with a trayful of rapidly cooling food may have your seat. There is no tipping at a fast food restaurant.

When you use the drive-through window where you call your order into a speaker, have your order ready before you begin. As a courtesy to cars behind you, this is not the time to ponder choices. Especially when you have a carful of children, take their orders *before* you get to the window so you can place the complete order quickly.

6

Especially for Guests:

Please and Thank You and Everything in Between

There are some people who seem to be on everybody's guest list—who have that certain "something" that makes them a host's delight. That "something" is simply the ability to accept hospitality with charm, grace and impeccable manners. It is found in the guest who is cordial to other guests, who does not make impossible demands, who lends a hand quietly, neither needing to be asked nor taking charge. And it is found in the guest who responds to an invitation promptly, with real pleasure or with sincere regret.

YOU ARE CORDIALLY INVITED. . .

A properly worded invitation helps guests anticipate the event to which they are invited. Whether a telephone call to say, "Harry just arrived home from Novia Scotia with half a salmon which we're poaching right now—we're hoping you can come over tonight about 6:30 and share it with us!" or a third-person, formal invitiation that begins, "The honour of your presence is requested. . . ," the invitation has its own guidelines.

A spur-of-the-moment invitation is never worded, "What

are you doing this evening?" or "Are you busy tonight?" which leaves the potential guest uncertain of how to reply. Guests certainly want to know *why*: If the host is planning a viewing of three hours of videotape from her family's vacation in the mountains, he may wish to decline this opportunity. If the host is planning, instead, a casual dinner among friends, the invitation may be more appealing. But if the intent of the invitation isn't stated immediately, the reply is difficult. It is awkward to ask, "Why do you want to know?" but often this is the only recourse. The breach of etiquette is really being committed by the host in not saying, "I know this is last minute, but John was just sent a case of prime steaks by a client and we'd love to share them with you—are you free to come to dinner tonight?"

Guidelines for invitations to more formal occasions are those of form and content, as well. Like any other type of correspondence, the invitation is a reflection of the host, and it is time well spent to select invitations that convey the formality or mood of the event.

Third-Person Formal Invitations

Formal invitations, although rare for private dinners, are engraved or printed on white or cream cards—either plain or bordered by a plate mark (a raised border in the paper). The size of the card of invitation varies with personal preference. The most graceful proportion is approximately three units in height to four in width, or four high by three wide. Cards may vary in size from 6 by 4 1/2 to 4 by 3 inches. United States postal regulations require mailing envelopes be at least 3 1/2 inches high by 5 inches wide. Invitations smaller than this size must still be mailed in envelopes that comply with postal regulations.

The lettering is a matter of personal choice, but the plainer the design, the safer. Punctuation is used only when words requir-

ing separation occur on the same line, and in certain abbrevia-
tions, such as "R.s.v.p." The time should never be given as nine-
thirty, but as "half past nine o'clock," or the more conservative
form, "half after nine o'clock."

Traditionally the phrases "black tie" or "white tie" were never
used on invitations to weddings or private parties. It was
assumed that people receiving formal invitations to these events
would know what to wear. Today, however, the vast majority of
parties are *not* formal, so the hostess who wishes her guests to
dress formally must indicate this on her invitations. The phrase
"black tie" should appear in the lower right-hand corner of invitations to proms, charity balls, formal dinners or dances,
evening weddings, or any event to which a wide assortment of
people are invited.

> *Mr. and Mrs. Donald Coleman*
> *request the pleasure of your company*
> *at dinner*
> *on Saturday, the twenty-first of July*
> *at half past seven o'clock*
> *Millstone Lane*
> *Southampton, New York 11968*
> *R.s.v.p.*   *Black Tie*

Handwritten Formal Invitations

When the formal invitation to dinner or luncheon is written
instead of engraved, plain white or cream notepaper or paper
stamped with the house address is used. The wording and spac-
ing must follow the engraved models exactly. The invitation
must be written by hand, not typewritten.

Mr. and Mrs. Frank Kemp
request the pleasure of
Mr. and Mrs. Robert Armao's
company at dinner
on Saturday, the sixth of February
at eight o'clock
The Darien Yacht Club

R.s.v.p.
22 Seabreeze Road
Darien, Connecticut 06820

The Fill-In Invitation

Hostesses who entertain frequently and formally often have a supply of fill-in cards printed that can be used for any occasion.

Dr. and Mrs. Barry Farnham
request the pleasure of
Mr. and Mrs. Albert Cardinali's
company at dinner
on Saturday, the third of October
at eight o'clock
324 Midland Avenue
Princeton Junction, New Jersey 08850

If there is a guest of honor, "to meet Mrs. William Barrett" is handwritten at the top.

Semiformal Fill-In Cards

For most mailed invitations, a fill-in card is appropriate, easy to use and attractive. These are found at most card and gift stores or can be ordered through a stationer. The printed lines follow the wording of the formal third-person invitations making it convenient for the hostess to fill in her information. After "For" would be written dinner, or a cocktail buffet, or whatever the purpose of the invitation is, and all other pertinent information would be added. Some fill-in cards do not have an "R.s.v.p." printed at the bottom. It may be added, with a telephone number written after when the hostess is soliciting telephone responses, or it may say "regrets only."

Invitations to a formal or large dinner party should be extended between two and three weeks ahead of time, especially during busy social seasons. Invitations to informal and casual dinners may be totally spontaneous and issued by telephone, or sent at least a week in advance if written.

Handwritten Notes

A personal invitation might be used to invite someone to a particularly special event. It could read:

Dear Liz and Charles,

Will you come to lunch on Saturday the tenth at half past twelve to meet Lisa's fiancé, Frank O'Gorman?

I hope so much that you will be able to join us.

Affectionately,

Lynn

It is written on personal notepaper and mailed anywhere from one to two weeks beforehand.

R.S.V.P.-ING

Anyone receiving an invitation with an R.s.v.p. on it is *obliged* to reply as promptly as possible. It is inexcusably rude to leave someone who has invited you to a party with no idea of how many people to expect.

Your reply should match the invitation. A formal, third-person invitation requires a third-person reply. However, a good friend who wishes to explain her refusal or to express her delight in the invitation may always write a personal note if she prefers. Those who groan at the thought of written replies should stop and think how much easier it is to follow the prescribed third-person form than to compose a lengthier letter. The form of a third-person affirmative reply is:

Dr. and Mrs. Eugene Wasserman
accept with pleasure
the kind invitation of
Dr. and Mrs. Ben Glassman
for dinner
on Monday, the tenth of December
at eight o'clock

Also used, but not quite so formal, is this form:

Mr. and Mrs. Richard King
accept with pleasure
Dr. and Mrs. Frank Kilduff's
kind invitation for dinner
on Thursday, the twelfth of June
at eight o'clock

If you must regret an invitation, you would write:

Mr. and Mrs. Peter Roggemann
regret that they are unable to accept
the kind invitation of
Mr. and Mrs. Marcus Moore
for Friday, the thirtieth of May

If one half of a couple is able to accept but the other must regret an invitation, the wording is:

Mrs. Frederick Wolgast
accepts with pleasure
Mr. and Mrs. Clay's
kind invitation for
Saturday, the second of October
but regrets that
Mr. Wolgast
will be unable to attend

If it were the wife who could not attend, the wording would merely transpose the "Mr." and "Mrs." If the invitation is addressed to both members of an unmarried couple who are living together, they may respond in the same way.

When an R.s.v.p. is followed by a telephone number, do your best to telephone your answer. If you cannot get through to the host after several attempts, however, do not give up. Rather than no reply at all, he will appreciate a brief note or even a postcard saying "We'll be there" or "So sorry, can't make it."

If the invitation says "regrets only," don't send or call an acceptance unless you have something to discuss with the hostess. If there is no R.s.v.p. at all, you are not obligated to reply, but it is never *wrong* to do so, and any hostess will appreciate your effort.

You are never obligated to accept an invitation. Once having accepted however, you must go. Nothing can change an acceptance to a regret except illness, death in the family, or a sudden, unavoidable trip.

Furthermore, having refused an invitation on these grounds, you must not accept another more desirable one for the same day. You need give no excuse beyond, "I'm afraid we are busy on the twelfth," and *that* leaves you free to accept anything else that comes along. But if you have refused because you would be "out of town" and then you appear at a party attended by a mutual friend, you can certainly give up any idea of friendship with the senders of the first invitation.

Changing Your Answer

If for any reason you find you cannot attend a function that you have already accepted, it is essential that you let the hostess know immediately. Not to do so at once would be inconsiderate since she will want time to invite others in your place. Even at a large catered party it is important, because the hostess pays for the number of guests expected, not for how many actually arrive. In the case of an open house or a big cocktail party, it is not so much a practical matter as it is one of common courtesy.

In most cases a telephone call is best, as it is quick and gives you a chance to explain your problem and express your regrets. If you prefer, however, and there is ample time, you may write a short note, giving the reason and your apologies.

Sometimes a person refuses an invitation for perfectly legitimate reasons and then finds that circumstances have changed and he can attend after all. If the affair is a party involving a limited number, such as for bridge, a theater party or a seated dinner, he must swallow his disappointment and hope to be asked again. The hostess will surely have filled his place, and it would only embarrass her if he asked to be "reinstated." However, if the party is a large reception, a cocktail buffet, a picnic or any affair at which another guest or two would not cause any complications, he may call the hostess, explain his situation and ask if he may change his regret to an acceptance.

Asking for an Invitation

One may never ask for an invitation for oneself anywhere. Nor does one ask to bring an extra person to a meal unless one knows it is a buffet at which one or two unexpected people might make no difference.

When regretting an invitation you may always explain that you are expecting to have weekend guests. Ordinarily the hostess-to-be says "I'm sorry!" But if it happens that she is having a big buffet lunch or a cocktail party she may say, "Do bring them, I'd love to meet them."

Requests for invitations are almost always telephoned, so that the invitee's situation can be explained, and the hostess can also explain her "Of course" or "I'm sorry you won't be able to join us."

When One Can and One Can't

There are times when it is acceptable to regret an invitation for one member of a couple and accept for the other. These times include weddings, bar or bat mitzvahs and large cocktail parties or buffet dinners. There are other times, however, when it is not. When tickets are to be ordered for a show following dinner, when a hostess is making up a table of bridge, or when a hostess has a definite seating plan in mind and it is based on the invitation to couples, you must regret for both by saying, "Thank you so much for thinking of us—we would love to come but Jack will be in Seattle on business that weekend." If the hostess doesn't mind changing her numbers, or finding another fourth for bridge, or asking someone else to share the fourth ticket for the show, she will say so. If she does mind, or she can't do this, then she will express her sincere regret and hope that you can get together soon.

"What May I Bring?"

This question should never be asked when responding to an invitation to a formal dinner, but may certainly be asked of a friend inviting you to a barbecue or a family party. If your hostess takes you up on your offer, you, of course, must follow through and provide the bottle of wine or plate of brownies or bag of ice cubes or whatever she asks. If she suggests an hors d'oeuvre, you obviously would not be the last to arrive at the party!

WHAT TO WEAR

An area of great insecurity for guests is that of attire. Even with universally relaxed dress codes, there still are simple rules of dress that should alleviate that insecurity.

If the invitation is formal, so is the attire. For women, a cocktail-length dress, a dressy suit, or dressy pants with complementing blouse, skirt, or jacket is appropriate. For men, a dark suit, preferably dark gray or dark blue, and a shirt and tie are worn. In some areas, formal means black tie—if you aren't sure, ask your hostess if the event is black-tie for men. If so, a tuxedo or dinner jacket would be worn.

If the invitation states "casual," then shorts in the summer, slacks and sweaters in the fall and winter, sandals, loafers, skirts and blouses, short-sleeved sports shirts and other clothing of that ilk may be worn.

For anything in between, men may safely wear a blazer or sports jacket and slacks with a shirt and tie. Women may wear a sportswear dress or separates, cotton or linen in warm weather, wool in cooler weather. The time of day determines how much accessorizing is required to dress an ensemble up or down. A brunch is less dressy than a buffet dinner, for example.

Naturally, invitations to such entertainments as a pool party and lunch indicate sports attire and the inclusion of a swimsuit in your bag. I would not recommend *wearing* your swimsuit, however. I have been invited to any number of pool parties where no one swam, let alone appeared in a bathing suit. Whether suffering selfconsciousness or insecurity about what to do, everyone at these parties stood decoratively around the pool in the clothes they came in, and went home. In reality it is up to the host to announce that it is time to swim, show everyone to a changing room and be the first in the pool in order for guests to feel comfortable following "suit."

WHEN TO ARRIVE

To me, the time given on an invitation is the time a host expects his guests to arrive. The concept of being "fashionably late" has given rise to great guest anxiety, even to the extent of a couple driving quickly past their host's house because they see no other cars yet. In some parts of the country, the hostess might be still in her robe and hot rollers at the time she has indicated on the invitation that the party will begin, knowing that no one will actually show up for at least thirty minutes.

No matter how late may be fashionable in your town, fifteen minutes is the very latest you should be to any party, particularly to a dinner party. Naturally, open houses, by their very nature, are places where people come and go right up to a few minutes before they are over, but a planned dinner party has a certain agenda, such as an hour for cocktails, followed by dinner, that should be respected by guests. No caring guest should cause inconvenience to his hostess by arriving very late without notice that he will do so, and no caring host should be put in the position of inconveniencing his other guests by forcing them to wait interminably for late arrivers.

When you do get lost, have a flat tire or break the heel on your shoe, causing your delay, you should call, if at all possible, and apologize profusely upon arrival. If you are able to call and know you will be later still, you should tell your hostess to proceed without you; that you will catch up as soon as you arrive.

HOSTESS GIFTS

In some areas of the country, no guests would dream of arriving at anyone's door without a gift in hand. If you live in such a place, then common sense should be your guide when it comes to selecting a gift to take to your hosts.

Never arrive with an unanticipated course for dinner. When your hostess has spent the afternoon preparing a strawberry rhubarb tart, she will not be pleased to have to serve your chocolate cake or assorted Italian pastries. Gifts of food are fine if they are croissants and jam for breakfast or a small box of chocolates. If you do arrive with something like a plate of lemon squares or a chocolate cake, you must say, "This is for you and the family tomorrow," so it is very clear that you are *not* expecting to see it on the dinner table.

Try to avoid arriving with an armful of cut flowers, as well. A busy hostess will have to scurry to find a vase, stop to give the stems a fresh cut and then arrange the flowers, all tasks she would ordinarily love, but not when she is also answering the door and seeing to her guests' comfort. A potted flowering plant or flowers already arranged are fine. If you do arrive with cut flowers, then you should say immediately, "Tell me where to find a vase and I'll arrange these for you." If it is spring and you are surrounded by lilacs that you would like to share, you can also call ahead to see if your hostess would like an armful. In this case, she has time to get a vase out and ready for your gift. When you are the guest of honor, a flower arrangement delivered by a florist on the day of the party is a lovely gesture of your appreciation.

Wine, liquor and liqueurs are acceptable gifts, as are small gifts for small children in the house, or any number of small and thoughtful items, from a tiny book on drying herbs for a friend who has a gardenful to a tape you have made of favorite songs you think your host will enjoy.

A thank-you call or note from the guest is nice but not obligatory. The host or hostess who receives a gift need make no further acknowledgement than, "Thank you, we'll look forward to enjoying this," at the time of presentation.

WHEN DINNER IS ANNOUNCED

When dinner is announced, be a thoughtful guest and don't ignore the invitation, sitting back and sipping slowly at your full cocktail glass. There is nothing that makes a hostess feel more helpless than those recalcitrant guests who will not respond to her call to dinner. The group that continues to stand on the patio drinking and talking, the twosome who smile but don't respond—these are rude people who are forgetting that they are accepting someone's hospitality when the only demand she has put on them is to come to dinner. If a buffet dinner is being served and the line is long, it certainly is permissible to wait a few minutes just where you are rather than queuing up, but that few minutes should not extend into very many. Recall that your hostess cannot eat until she sees that everyone is served, so you are being thoughtless of her in yet another way.

You will earn her gratitude, and that of other hungry but shyer guests, if you will even lead the way to the buffet when dinner is called instead of hanging back and waiting for someone else to be first. Just don't jump up and fly out as if you have been kept waiting to the point of starvation. Watch your hostess, and if she seems to be edging toward the door, take one more sip and rise.

WATCH THE FORK

In most instances, guests do not begin eating until their hostess "raises her fork," or begins eating herself. There are times, such as at a dinner where the host or hostess is serving and it is a long process, when she would say, "Please begin eating so that your food doesn't get cold," or whatever, to encourage guests to start without her. When three or more are served in this manner, in fact, any one of them may begin eating, on the premise that the hostess has neglected to encourage him to do so. There have been times when guests have begun eating before everyone was served only to have the host ask for grace to be said. It is generally more comfortable to wait for the hostess's fork, or for her words instructing you to eat, before you do.

At a restaurant, all the guests at one table wait to eat until everyone at the table has received his or her food. In a good restaurant, everyone will be served at once so the wait is not long. When two out of four diners are served and the other two plates seem nowhere in sight, the two who have not been served should be sure to tell those who have to please go ahead and begin.

WHEN YOU DON'T EAT CERTAIN FOODS

For years I have suggested that guests with dietary restrictions not mention it to their hostess when invited to dinner. This advice holds, when the restrictions are mild or self-imposed. If you are watching your weight, you would not say "I'll come, but I'm not eating anything with a cream sauce." If not a fan of broccoli, you would not say "You're on notice that I really hate broccoli." You simply would eat what you could and take very small portions or nothing of that which you chose not to eat.

When you are on a strict medical diet, however, or if you follow a kosher diet, or are a vegetarian, you must mention it before arriving at the door. You would say, "Deirdre, I would love to come to dinner, but you should know I have become a vegetarian. I would imagine you are serving salad or vegetables or potatoes or pasta of some sort, which is just perfect for me—I will only come if you promise you won't change your menu or fix something special for me." Or, "Kate, the doctor has me on a really restricted diet, so if I could bring my own dinner to heat up in the kitchen I would love to be there with you and your other guests. If that is a problem, I'll have to pass this time and we'll get together later."

When you have a severe allergy to some foods, you must say so before accepting the invitation. People who become seriously ill when they eat certain foods owe it to a potential hostess to say so. "Ruth, Bob and I would love to come, but he is terribly allergic to anything with eggs in it. If this is a problem we had better decline this time, but hope you will think of us again."

No hostess who prepares a lovely meal wants to know at the last minute that a guest can't eat it. If she knows ahead of time, she can have something on the menu that he can eat, and will tell him about those things that he should not eat.

If you arrive at the door and announce blithely, "Oh, by the way, I am now a vegetarian," or "I'm not going to eat; I'm on a really special diet, but I'll sit with everyone," you are doing your hostess a grave injustice. Don't put your hostess in the position of trying to think of what she could prepare quickly for you.

WHERE IS THE, UH...

There is nothing embarrassing about asking where the bathroom is. You may call it the bathroom, the washroom, the powder room or even the lavatory. Don't call it the "little girls' room" or the "little boys' room" which is sophomoric and ridiculous.

If you don't know where the bathroom is, ask your hostess, "May I use your bathroom?" She will, of course, say yes and if she doesn't tell you where it is, say, "Could you point me in the right direction?" It really seems silly to ask permission to use the bathroom, since no one is going to refuse, so it is equally acceptable just to ask, "Jane, could you point me in the direction of the bathroom?" with no permission preamble.

If you know where it is, just go. While you're there, you may *not* open cabinets and cupboards or snoop through bedrooms on the way.

When you are finished, make sure you have flushed and

wiped the sink of any spilled powder or other mess you may have created.

Hand towels are to be used after you wash your hands. Do not fold them back neatly in thirds when finished; rather fold them loosely and rehang them on the rack. If paper towels are provided, they are thrown in the wastebasket after use, not left on the edge of the sink.

Probably more embarrassing to most people than asking where the bathroom is is asking where the toilet paper is. I don't know why, really, since the embarrassment is more the hostess's for having left something undone. It is a good idea to check that it is available before locking yourself into the bathroom. If the roll is empty and a fresh roll is not in sight, find your hostess and ask her quietly where you can find a roll of toilet tissue, since there is none in the bathroom.

WHERE'S THE KETCHUP?

A hostess who has put dishes of steak sauce and spicy mustard on the table to accompany a barbecued steak may be asked if she has any ketchup. A hostess who has not put accompanying sauces on the table may not be asked, no matter how much you like to cover your steak in it. If she felt sauces were required, she would have provided them. Obviously, she does not, perhaps wanting guests to taste the flavors of the marinade or the delicate balance of her herbed carrots and parsleyed beef.

GROOMING

All grooming is done in the bathroom, never at the table. Do not peer into a compact, run a comb through your crew cut, or dip your napkin in your ice water to wipe a spot off your chin. Excuse yourself and tend to these needs in private. A touch of lipstick is all that should be applied at the table if you can do so discretely.

HOW CAN I HELP?

Probably the best help you can give a hostess is to have a wonderful time. You can ask her what you can do to be of assistance, suggesting that you could fill the water goblets, for instance. If she says, "Thank you, but there's really nothing to do right now," you may reply, "Then please let me know as soon as there is a way I can help." No matter how much you want to help, don't follow her to the kitchen unless invited to do so. Or when she rises to clear the table, don't jump up to help unless she has asked you to beforehand.

When you are asked to help, do precisely what is asked and no more.

At a dinner served by a maid or butler, guests never try to help by handing them empty plates, stacking dishes, etc. An exception is a large restaurant table where the waiter cannot reach all of the places. In that case, a guest may take the plate from the waiter and pass it to the person beyond the waiter's reach. Guests do not talk to servants at a formal dinner other than to say "No, thank you" or possibly to request something that the hostess is not aware of. Of course, if you know a servant well and have not seen her (or him) before a small dinner, you would greet her briefly when she passes something to you, saying: "Good evening, Mary—nice to see you" or whatever you wish.

Regardless of whether or not a hostess has help, do not insist on clearing the table and washing the dishes. If the dinner is formal, or you are somewhat of a stranger, you should not even make the offer. At a more casual dinner you may ask, "Can't we help clean up?" If the hostess refuses help, don't insist or get up and do it anyway. Respect her wishes, relax and enjoy yourself.

WHOOPS!

The topic of spills and accidental damage is covered elsewhere in this book, from the point of view of the host with mention of the obligation of the guest who spills or breaks something. It bears addressing once more. Presumably any spill or breakage caused by you is accidental. You must offer to clean up a spill, although your hostess will likely wish to take care of it herself, and you must, at a later time, offer to pay for any damage. Do not carry on all evening. One heartfelt apology is all that is needed.

HOST PETS

Sometimes your hosts allow their pets to roam around the dinner table, looking expectantly at guests who may possibly drop a tender morsel to them. The pets should not be there, but when they are, no matter how adoringly they gaze at you, do not feed them at the table. It could be that they are not allowed table scraps and you might be upsetting their training, so your decision to slip them something would not be a good one. Ideally, your host, seeing that Max the Australian kelpie was getting the better of his guests, would take him out of the room. You really should ignore the dog, as tempting as it may be to rid yourself of dreaded cauliflower or a piece of fatty meat so it doesn't remain on your plate.

CHECKING OUT THE CHINA

A polite guest does not examine the silver for a hallmark or casually turn a dish at the table upside down to investigate the quality of the china, any more than she runs her gloved finger over the mantle for dust. Nothing more need be said than "Don't do it."

SMOKING

Do not light a cigarette in someone's home without asking permission to do so first of the host and then of the others in the room. Don't even ask if you do not see an ashtray in sight. If in need of a cigarette, you may, in an aside to your host or hostess, say, "Do you mind if I step outside for a cigarette?" She will either happily show you the way or locate an ashtray if she doesn't mind your smoking in the house.

Cigar and pipe smokers, unless in a roomful of like-minded individuals, should save that pleasure for when they go home. While cigarette smoke does not bother some people, cigar and pipe smoke bothers most people.

Even if smoking is permitted and there are ashtrays on the table, cigarettes should not be lighted until coffee is served. I once sat next to a very fast eater. While I was barely halfway through my first course, he had finished his and lit a cigarette. This was unpleasant to all of us in his vicinity. He should not have smoked between courses unless his host and/or hostess was doing so and other guests did not mind.

UNDER SIEGE

It sometimes happens that someone decides he doesn't like you and becomes belligerent about it, shouting, poking his finger into your chest or arguing vigorously. Your best move is to extricate yourself politely and quickly move into another group. If need be, excuse yourself and go to the bathroom for a few minutes in hopes that he is not lying in wait when you exit.

If the agressive behavior does not stop and you feel truly under siege, you must seek your host and ask for assistance. It is his responsibility to ask the offensive one to stop or to leave if he can't control his behavior.

SECONDS

However hearty your appetite, don't heap your plate with piles of food. Take regular-sized portions and go back for seconds, at a buffet, or wait to be offered seconds at a seated dinner. Note, however, that you may not ask for seconds at a formal dinner, although you may at an informal one. At a formal dinner where second helpings should be offered, the hostess rings for a server and asks, "Would you please pass the meat and rice again?" If there are no helpers and the host has served the entrée from a sideboard, he or the hostess usually urges guests to pass their plates to the host for a second helping. To do this, leave the silver on the plate, making sure it is not right on the edge. Never hold your flatware in your hand or put it on the tablecloth when you pass your plate.

As a courtesy when only one person takes a second helping, a considerate hostess takes a little too so that her guest will not feel self-conscious or feel that she is responsible for holding everyone up.

AND HE SAID, SHE SAID...

No matter how much you love to gossip or talk about others, curb your desire to do so at a party, for a few reasons. First, it is impolite. Second, you never know who knows the person you are talking about with such relish, or worse yet, may be related to her. Third, you don't want to be thought of as someone who talks about other people. There are many who would dread leaving the room in fear that you will make them the target of your next barb. There are many more interesting things to talk about than other people, especially if you're talking about them in a derogatory way. If what you have to say is nothing but praise and accolades, by all means proceed.

HELLO *THERE*

I dislike being called "There." I have a name, and I am happy to tell anyone who has forgotten it what it is. I am not unique in this feeling, and certainly am forgiving of those who don't remember, particularly at a large party when one is introduced to many new people. When you find yourself face to face with someone to whom you have been introduced but whose name you have forgotten, say so. Say, "You'll have to forgive me but I can't remember your name. Please tell me again what it is."

By the same token, when you recognize that someone has forgotten your name, don't be huffy but rather offer it—"We met earlier. I'm Elizabeth Post." If you wish, you can go on and add a modifying sentence—"My husband, Bill, and I are visiting Helen this weekend," or "Helen and I were in college together and have managed to keep in touch ever since."

TABLE TALK

It is the responsibility of every guest to do his and her best to engage in conversation with table mates. If the person to your left is sitting in miserable silence, try hard to get her to talk. If she is impossibly shy, involve the person to her left and attempt a three-way conversation, or the person across the table, if it isn't too wide. No matter how fascinating the person to your right may be, you are obligated to turn to your left periodically and talk to a perhaps less mesmerizing conversationalist on your other side.

Long ago, the "turning of the table" was designed to make people divide their conversation time more or less evenly between their two dinner companions. The hostess, after the first two courses (or any time she chose), would turn from the man on her right to the one on her left, and each woman at the table was supposed to notice this and switch at the same time. This was certainly a forced means of achieving a change that should happen naturally at a convenient break in the conversation rather than at a signal. This is no longer a custom. The rule that remains is that you must at some time during dinner talk to both your neighbors.

Other rules are self-evident. A popular guest does not talk at length about himself, he is not didactic but listens to his neighbors' point of view, and he does not, at length, at least, talk shop.

Shop talk can dampen any party unless everyone there is involved in the same business, sport or hobby. Have you ever been to a party on a Saturday night, where most of the men had played golf that day? If you were not an ardent golfer yourself, you might as well have stayed home with a good book. In short, any guest who talks continually about one subject, regardless of the listener's interest, can only be classified as a bore.

BEING A NO-SHOW

The only reasons for backing out of an acceptance are a death, illness or unexpected travel plans, as mentioned before. Never cancel on a hostess because you have received a better offer or because you just don't feel like going. Once having accepted the invitation, your obligation is to honor it with your presence.

Along the same lines, it is inexcusably rude to arrive at a dinner or other party and leave after the second course, unless stricken with an illness. Those who party-hop without telling their hostesses they must do so are, at the least, inconsiderate. If you are invited somewhere and know that you will have to leave at a certain time for another engagement, you must say so at the time of the invitation. "Kay, we'd love to be at your cocktail party, but we are expected somewhere for dinner at eight." If Kay says, "Then please come and stay as long as you can," you certainly may do so. If she says, "That's too bad, we would have loved to have seen you," you'll know your coming-and-going doesn't work for her.

NO COASTERS

A last-minute detail often overlooked by hosts and hostesses is the placement of coasters around the room. You should not put your glass down on a wooden surface or on a book or even on a magazine; but rather you should simply ask your hostess for a coaster. If she says, "Just put it right on the table," then of course you may.

WHAT'S IN THERE?

While a host may offer to tour a guest through his apartment, house or grounds, a guest should not request a tour. Many a harried hostess has thrown all the laundry on the floor or didn't have time to make beds or straighten up, and the last thing she would want would be for guests to see the examples of her disarray. You may admire the room you are in, the view from the sixty-fifth floor, the beautiful landscaping around the front door or anything else that is in your line of vision, but you may not ask to see more.

TO YOUR HEALTH!

When you are the guest of honor and a toast is proposed, in your honor, you do not drink with the others, nor, if at a formal event, do you rise when they do. You remain seated, and raise your glass to acknowledge their tribute. You may, if you wish, after everyone is seated, rise yourself and propose a response toast.

When at an informal gathering, it is usual for the host to be the first to propose a toast, to his guests, to his wife, to his significant other, to the occasion for which they are all gathered or just "to good friends." After the host has proposed this toast, guests may propose those of their own.

If you don't drink wine or champagne, you should still join in any toast that is proposed, with your water goblet or beverage glass of any sort raised in participation.

SAYING GRACE

When you are the guest at a dinner table where grace is said, you should join in, if comfortable doing so. If your religion or your personal beliefs do not permit you to do so, you at least bow your head and sit quietly through the prayer. A host should never ask a guest to say grace unless that guest is a member of the clergy. If asked, however, "Ken, would you say grace?" you should either do your best, or, if you simply cannot think of a thing to say or would prefer not to, say, "Thank you, Joe, but I'd rather you said it for us." Shaking your head, looking horrified, or just saying, "No, I won't," aren't good responses, even though you are the one being put on the spot.

OUT ON THE TOWN

When invited to a club or restaurant for lunch or dinner or tea or whatever by a friend, the implication is that you are her guest. When she says, "Sally, are you free to have lunch with me on the twentieth," or "Joanne, I'm hoping you will be my guest for tea at the Plaza on Friday," she means just that. In this circumstance, you do not grab the check and insist that it is really your treat. Do not, either, insist that you will leave the tip or that you will pay your share. These financial arrangements are saved for a time when you agree, jointly, to meet for lunch and each pay your own way. This time, accept her hospitality with thanks and reciprocate some other time.

It is far better to clarify the finances before entering a restaurant so that there is no bickering or insistence when the check is delivered. This haggling, although done with the best intentions and the sincere desire to have another be your guest or vice versa, should not to be done across a table or in front of a cashier.

When you have invited someone to be your guest and she tries to pay, be firm and say, "Thank you so much, Peg, but this is my party. You can treat me some other time."

WHAT TO ORDER

When you are someone's guest in a restaurant, it is often tricky to know what to order, particularly since the host so often says, "What will you have?" before indicating what he is having. This is not so much a matter of cost as it is one of courses. If you order an appetizer, salad and entrée and your host orders soup and salad only, you feel embarrassed. If you just order soup and a sandwich and your host orders a three-course lunch, you feel foolish.

If your host gives no indication of how he is ordering, ask. Say, "Tom, what do you recommend?" on the assumption that he has been in the restaurant before. Or, if he hasn't, "What do you think sounds good?" You do this in hopes that he responds by saying, "I think I'll have the medallions of veal and the mixed green salad," rather than by saying, "Gosh, I don't know!" You can actually ask, "Tom, what are you having?" if feeling particularly unsure. It is his responsibility to offer this information first, to make you comfortable, but if he doesn't, you should have no qualms about requesting it.

THANK YOU VERY MUCH!

Whatever the entertainment, however good or bad a time you had, you must express your thanks. You thank your host and hostess at the door when you leave, and it is thoughtful to call the next day and thank them again, remarking on some detail of the party, whether the food or the company or the fresh flowers, or all three. You also may write a thank-you note after being entertained, to express once again the pleasure you experienced and your thanks for a lovely evening, or afternoon, or whatever. It is redundant to both call and write, so choose one and be sincere in your thanks. Even if you disliked the dinner or found their other friends utterly boring, you surely can find one or two things to exclaim about and be thankful for.

You also call or write thanks to a friend who has entertained you in a restaurant or at her club, again mentioning something memorable and expressing your pleasure.

PAYING BACK

All invitations must be returned in some form or another. When a couple invites you to a restaurant for dinner, you needn't return the invitation in kind though, of course, you may. You might instead have them to your home for brunch or take them to a baseball game (assuming they are enthusiasts) or to the ballet.

People who have been invited to a great many parties and haven't the time or the energy to give a number of small parties sometimes repay their obligations by inviting everyone to whom they are indebted at once. The result is guests are not chosen for compatibility, there are not enough chairs, the crowd is so large that no one can move about freely, and the noise level reaches a deafening pitch. If you incur social obligations with any frequency, make the effort to give small parties from time to time and avoid the necessity of a yearly, and not very much fun, "pay-back."

A GUEST OF THE COMPANY

When social gatherings are sponsored by the company or hosted by your spouse's employer, you are, naturally, the model guest: polite, sociable, thoughtful and in all ways representing yourself and your spouse as attractive people. At the table your manners are impeccable, for, believe it or not, more promotions have been won or lost on someone's table manners or, perhaps unfairly, his or her spouse's manners, at the table than for all other reasons combined.

Because much of business today revolves around perfect conduct and sometimes social entertaining, it is important to the management of any company to be sure their top management candidates will not embarrass them in public.

Not only should anyone at a business function around a meal table use his or her very best manners, he or she should remember them the next day, too, with a thank-you note. When a spouse is included, it is often nice if he or she writes the note, thanking his or her spouse's boss for including him (or her) and for a lovely time.

AFTER DINNER

Guests do not put their napkins on the table until their hostess does. When she rises to signal the end of the meal, they do not prolong their conversation, but rise and go wherever she indicates.

If games are suggested after dinner, no matter how you feel about them, try to look as though you think it's a fine idea and help your hostess to organize the group. Very often, especially if the guests do not have a great deal in common, entertainment that a hostess would ordinarily avoid can be the means of pulling a party together and making a delightful evening out of what started out as a very dull one.

FREE ADVICE

When you are a guest in someone's home or at someone's table, you must not ever take advantage of any professionals you meet. It is true that strong business deals and partnerships are begun between strangers who meet at someone's table, but it is also true that one of the most intrusive things you can do is to try and get free advice from a doctor, dentist, lawyer, interior designer, bricklayer or accountant.

Think about it. If you were a dentist, having spent a long week peering into eighty or one hundred mouths, would you be pleased if, at a dinner party, someone you just met opened up so you could advise him on his left rear molar? I think not.

If you were a lawyer, would you appreciate having a new acquaintance corner you with a long tale of legal woes and ask for your ruling on who was right and who was wrong? No, you wouldn't.

If you meet a professional you like, ask for his business card or his number and you can call the office the next business day to make an appointment. It is unthinkable for a guest to try to solicit free advice for personal problems or medical questions from another guest. In saying this, I am assuming that friends of the professional person would not do this, ever, and that it is only strangers who would be so presumptuous.

It is far better to ask a physician you meet what he thinks of a world crisis or the latest movie or a television series on gardening than to discuss your gallbladder with him. It is a temptation to bring up a topic related to his profession, even if you aren't asking for advice, but it is one to resist.

When you are the guest with the specialty and another guest is cross-examining you or asking you to feel his kneecap or look at his bunion, you are well within your rights to say, "I'm off duty now, and can't even think about medical questions. I'd be happy to see you in my office if you would like to call tomorrow for an appointment, or to recommend a specialist to you who perhaps could help you."

DEPARTING

Once you have decided that it is time to go—GO! Nothing is more irritating than the guest who gets her coat, says good-bye to the other guests and twenty minutes later is still standing in the open door giving last-minute words of wisdom to her hostess.

Try to be sensitive and aware of the people around you. Most hostesses are reluctant to try to "speed the parting guest," so make an effort to observe when your hosts—and others at the party—begin to look tired, and make the move to break it up yourself. When there is a guest of honor, it is supposedly his or her obligation to leave first. But many do not know this, and furthermore they may be having a better time than some of the other guests and not want to leave as early. Fortunately, that old rule is obsolete, and with the exception of when the President of the United States is present, guests at a large party may leave whenever they wish. They should, however, remain for at least one hour after dinner, as it is hardly complimentary to the hostess to "eat and run." At a small party a couple should not leave long before anyone else seems ready to go, because their departure is very apt to break up the party. If they must leave early, they should explain that they have a young babysitter who must be home by nine-thirty, or a five A.M. flight the next day or whatever other reason excuses their early departure.

INDEX

Note: Numbers followed by *i* denote illustrations.

ABOUT THE AUTHOR

Elizabeth L. Post, granddaughter-in-law of the legendary Emily Post, has earned the mantel of her predecessor as America's foremost authority on etiquette. Mrs. Post has revised the classic *Etiquette* five times since 1965. In addition she has written *Emily Post's Complete Book of Wedding Etiquette, Emily Post's Wedding Planner, Emily Post's Table Manners for Today, Emily Post on Business Etiquette, Emily Post on Entertaining, Emily Post on Etiquette, Emily Post on Guests and Hosts, Emily Post on Invitations, Emily Post on Second Weddings, Please, Say Please, The Complete Book of Entertaining* with co-author Anthony Staffieri, and *Emily Post Talks with Teens about Manners and Etiquette* with co-author Joan M. Coles. Mrs. Post's advice on etiquette may also be found in the monthly column she writes for *Good Housekeeping* magazine, "Etiquette for Everyday."

Mrs. Post and her husband divide their time between homes in Florida and Vermont.